New Testament General Letters

Greg Kappas and Jared Nelms, EDS.

New Testament General Letters
Book Eight in TTI's Foundational Curriculum

© 2012 by The Timothy Initiative

International Standard Book Number: 978-1477582909

All rights reserved. Published and Printed in the United States of America.

Library of Congress Cataloging-in-Publication Data

No part of this book covered by the copyrights heron may be reproduced or copied
in any form or by any means without written permission of the publisher.

Scripture quotations are from: The New King James Version
Copyright © 1979, 1980, 1982 by Thomas Nelson, Inc.
Used by permission. All rights reserved.

First Edition-North America
Second Edition

ACKNOWLEDGEMENTS

TTI gives special gratitude to the Docent Group and the leadership of Glenn Lucke and Jared Wilson (Docent Executive Editor for this project). The Docent writer, Susan Miller did extensive work on this book and we are very grateful for her fine, thorough contribution. Rev. Lou Mancari spent hours upon hours editing this work and we extend our deepest appreciation to him.

TTI also gives thanks to Dr. David Nelms, our Founder/President for his vision and influence to see this New Curriculum written. Dr. Nelms has lived humbly to see you succeed greatly in Jesus Christ.

We express our gratitude for the fine, long editorial labor to TTI Executive Editor and Director, Dr. Greg Kappas and the Executive Editorial Assistant and International Director, Rev. Jared Nelms. In addition we thank the entire TTI editorial team of Dr. David Nelms, Rev. Jesse Nelms, Rev. Larry Starkey, Rev. Lou Mancari and Dr. David Nichols. Each of you has given such remarkable grace to us and now to these church planters.

TTI is greatly appreciative of the Grace Fellowship elders, pastors, administrative staff, leaders and GF family. TTI was birthed out of this "church for all nations." Thank you for your generosity in launching this exponential network of church planting movements.

TTI's Board of Directors has given us freedom and focus to excel still more. We are deeply moved by these men and women of God. Our TTI investor base of financial and prayer partners extend around the globe. These individuals, churches, ministries, networks, corporations and organizations are essential and strategic to our collective health and Kingdom impact. Thank you!

We thank the TTI Continental Directors, Regional Directors, National Directors and District/Training Center Leaders for your ministry of love and commitment. You are the ones that forge into new and current frontiers with the Gospel. You truly are our heroes.

Finally, we are forever grateful to you, the church planter. You are planting an orchard, a church planting center through your local church that will touch your region and the world with the Gospel of Jesus Christ. We are honored to serve the Lord Jesus Christ and you. You will make a difference for our great God as you multiply healthy churches for His glory. We love you and believe in you!

TTI Staff Team
September 2010

THE TIMOTHY INITIATIVE

*"What you have heard from me in the presence
of many witnesses entrust to faithful men
who will be able to teach others also."*

2 Timothy 2:2

This workbook is the eighth of 10 workbooks which assist in equipping church planting leaders to start churches that saturate a region and help reach every man, woman and child with the Good News of our Lord. Below is the list of this initial curriculum.

TTI Curriculum

Workbook Number/Course:

1. Hermeneutics

2. Homiletics

3. Church Planting (New Testament – Acts, Evangelism, Discipleship, Spiritual Life, T4T)

4. Old Testament 1

5. Old Testament 2

6. New Testament Gospels

7. New Testament Pastoral Epistles

8. New Testament General Letters

9. Major Bible Doctrines

10. Apologetics-Church History-Spiritual Warfare

Table of Contents

Introduction 9

Chapter 1: Romans 13

Chapter 2: 1 Corinthians 33

Chapter 3: 2 Corinthians 45

Chapter 4: Galatians 55

Chapter 5: Ephesians 63

Chapter 6: Philippians 73

Chapter 7: Colossians 81

Chapter 8: 1 Thessalonians 89

Chapter 9: 2 Thessalonians 97

Chapter 10: Philemon 101

Chapter 11: Hebrews 103

Chapter 12: James 121

Chapter 13: 1 Peter 131

Chapter 14: 2 Peter 137

Chapter 15: Letters of John 141

Chapter 16: Jude 149

Chapter 17: Revelation 155

Conclusion 177

Endnotes 179

INTRODUCTION

Roman rule changed the western world. Roads throughout the empire made travel easier than ever before. Cultures, philosophies and religions met in the cities along these roads. Latin and Greek became common languages. People freely mixed parts of one religion with parts of another. The Jewish people were only one of many ethnic groups the Romans governed. This is the setting into which Jesus Christ was born. This is the setting from which the church rose up. This is the setting writers of the New Testament wrote to.

The New Testament contains four different kinds of writings:

Gospels: *Matthew, Mark, Luke* and *John* record the life of Christ in their gospels. The Gospels are not complete biographies of Jesus. Rather, each Gospel writer has a different theme or purpose for writing. Sometimes stories overlap. Sometimes they are similar, but not identical (Book Five of the TTI Curriculum covers the Gospels in detail).

Acts: Luke wrote one of the Gospels, and then went on to write the book of *Acts*. This book tells the story of the early church and the spread of the Gospel (Book Three covers *Acts* and the lessons it holds for church growth).

Letters: Much of the New Testament is letters written to specific groups of Christians. Writers had specific situations in mind. As a group, letters from the apostle Paul are the "Pauline" letters. As a second group, letters by other church leaders are "general letters."

Vision: The book of Revelation stands alone in the New Testament. It is an example of *apocalyptic* literature. This is a Greek word that means "revelation." Apocalyptic literature arose among Jews and Christians to reveal certain mysteries about heaven and earth, mankind and God, angels and demons, the world today and the world to come. The Old Testament contains several examples of apocalyptic literature among the prophets, but *Revelation* is the only New Testament book of this type. *Revelation* uses visions, symbols and images that picture God's actions at the end of time.

This course covers most of the letters of the New Testament, and the mix of vision and prophecy in the book of *Revelation*.

Pauline Letters

The book of *Acts* records the death of Stephen, the first Christian martyr (*Act. 7:60*). After Stephen's death, persecution broke out in Jerusalem (*Act. 8:1*). Christians scattered to other parts of the Roman Empire. A young man named Saul dedicated himself to chasing Christians and bringing them back to Jerusalem for legal action. One of the Roman roads went northwest out of Jerusalem to Damascus. Saul was on this road when he had a vision of Jesus Christ (*Act. 9*). Saul believed, changed his name to Paul and became one of the great leaders of the church.

NOTES

God called Paul to take the good news of Jesus Christ to groups of people outside Jerusalem and beyond the Jewish people. Paul used the Roman system of roads for his travels to cities around the empire. On three long missionary trips, Paul started many churches, and the Gospel spread from there. The Pauline letters are writings of Paul to the first Christian churches. In most cases, both Jews and Gentiles who believed in Jesus were part of these churches.

We can divide Paul's letters into three types. First, Paul wrote letters during his missionary "journeys." These include *Galatians, 1 & 2 Thessalonians, 1 & 2 Corinthians* and *Romans*. The book of *Acts* traces Paul's three major missionary journeys. This information helps us understand the settings Paul was writing to and some key events. After Paul's third missionary journey, he became a Roman prisoner because of his Gospel preaching. He demanded his rights to a trial as a Roman citizen (see *Act. 25:1-11*), and spent two years as a prisoner in Rome waiting for trial. During this time, he wrote the "prison letters" of *Ephesians, Philippians, Colossians* and *Philemon*. We have hints in Paul's letters that perhaps he was released from prison and continued his ministry. Third, Paul wrote the "pastoral letters" of *1 & 2 Timothy* and *Titus*. He wrote these letters to young pastors to teach principles of leadership in the church (Book Seven covers this). Most likely, Paul was once again in prison late in life when he wrote the pastoral letters. Shortly after writing, he was executed.

General Letters

After the letters of Paul in the New Testament, we read a group of letters by various authors. Each writer uses a distinct writing style and vocabulary. Peter and John, two of Jesus' original disciples, wrote letters for Christians in churches to read. James and Jude were half-brothers of Jesus. They were not original disciples, but they became respected church leaders after Jesus' death and resurrection. The author of *Hebrews* is unknown. In some periods of church history, tradition suggested Paul wrote the book of *Hebrews*. However, the writing style and themes are very different from the Pauline letters, so it is doubtful that Paul wrote this letter. We simply do not know who the author is, but Christians accepted *Hebrews* as Scripture very early.

Revelation

John identifies himself as the author of *Revelation*. This is the same John who wrote the Gospel of *John* and the letters of *1, 2 & 3 John*. He was a disciple of Jesus. In his later years, John was a prisoner because of his preaching. He received the visions of *Revelation* while he was on Patmos, a prison island.

Dates of the Letters

The books of the New Testament appear in an order that becomes familiar to Christians. However, this is not the order in which the authors wrote. Most of the time, scholars cannot know exactly when each book was written. They use information found in the New Testament and historical events to decide when the writing probably happened. This is the most likely order in which writers produced the Pauline and general letters, as well as *Revelation*. Please refer to the chart on the following page:

Likely Order of New Testament Letters[1]:

James writes his letter	AD 46
Paul's first missionary journey	AD 47-49
Paul writes *Galatians*	AD 48
Paul's second missionary journey	AD 50-53
Paul writes *1 Thessalonians*	AD 51
Paul writes *2 Thessalonians*	AD 51-52
Paul's third missionary journey	AD 53-57
Paul writes *1 Corinthians*	AD 56 (April-May)
Paul writes *2 Corinthians*	AD 56 (September-October)
Paul writes *Romans*	AD 57
Paul is a prisoner in Rome	AD 60-62
Paul writes *Colossians*, *Ephesians*, *Philippians* and *Philemon*	AD 60-62
An unknown author writes *Hebrews* before this date	AD 64
Jude writes his letter	AD 60-64
Peter writes his first letter	AD 62-64
Peter writes his second letter	AD 64-67
Paul and Peter are executed in Rome	AD 67
John writes his letters	AD 90
John writes *Revelation*	AD 95
John dies	AD 100

How to Use This Manual

To get the most out of this course, be sure to do these things.

1. *Follow along in your Bible.* You'll find comments on selected phrases in the manual, but you must read the phrase in context to fully understand.

2. *Watch for key words and concepts.* At the beginning of each new chapter, look for the box that alerts you to key words and concepts in that New Testament book. Then as you study, look for the boxes that explain these ideas more fully.

3. *Look up cross-references.* After a comment on a verse, you may see references from other parts of the Bible. These will lead you to deeper study on specific points.

4. *Pause and reflect.* Throughout the manual, you will find sections that ask you to reflect on what you read. Other sections ask you to use your own words to explain what you are learning. Other sections help you organize main themes.

Above all else, let the Word of God speak to you with power. This manual is a tool to help you learn how to understand God's Word. Let God speak to you and change your life through what you learn.

Chapter One
ROMANS

The writings of Paul in the New Testament are letters to churches. Generally, Paul wrote to churches he visited. *Romans* is different. Paul did not go to Rome before he wrote this letter. Perhaps believers from Jerusalem moved to Rome after the Day of Pentecost and started the church. Paul planned to visit in the future and wanted the Romans to be ready for him.

Romans is the first letter from Paul to appear in the New Testament, but it was not the first letter he wrote. Paul probably wrote this letter from the city of Corinth in AD 57 or 58. He wrote during his third major missionary journey. During this trip, he collected money from churches to give to the poor in Jerusalem. Paul planned to take the money to Jerusalem. From there, he would go to Rome. He hoped to go to Spain also.

Paul used this letter to give a foundation for the Christian doctrine of salvation. The Roman church included both Jews and Gentiles. Paul explained the relationship between Jews and Gentiles in God's plan for salvation. The book of *Romans* presents spiritual truths in a clear system. The church in Rome had not yet received teaching from an apostle. Paul wanted to firmly establish them in the truth. He presented his themes in logical order. First Paul explained the need for salvation because humans are sinful. Then he explained how God provides salvation through Jesus. Then Paul explained new life in Christ. Throughout the book of *Romans*, Paul used quotations from the Old Testament to show that the same God the Jews knew in the Old Testament now brought salvation for all people.

Paul knew many people in the church (see *Romans 16*); He cared deeply for all of them. In addition to clear teaching, he gave them pastoral care. Paul dealt with problems between the Jews and Gentiles. Paul emphasized that they shared the great salvation God had given to all of them. Because of this, they should live in unity.

What to watch for:

Key words: Gospel, righteousness, justification, faith, salvation, law, sin, flesh, Spirit, grace, and called.

Key comparisons: law vs. grace, Adam vs. Christ, death vs. life, faith and works, life in the sinful self (flesh) vs. life in the Spirit.

1. Greetings and Prayer (*1:1-17*)

    A. Paul Identifies Himself (*1:1-2*)
- Paul is set apart for the Gospel as an apostle — "one who is sent."
- He is a willing servant. Paul uses the Hebrew sense of this word which is "one who serves out of love." (See *Exo. 21:5-6*).

    B. Jesus Is the Central Figure of the Gospel (*1:3-5*)
- The Resurrection proved that Jesus is God's Son.

C. <u>The Readers Are Saints, Holy Ones Set Apart for God</u> (*1:6-7*)

D. <u>Paul Thanks God for the Romans</u> (*1:8-17*)
- Paul often starts with thanksgiving to God for his readers. He thanks God that many people know about the faith of the Romans (*1:8-10*). What a great testimony for any group or individual Christian to have a faith that is "famous" — a faith that inspires others to embrace *the faith*.
- Paul longs to visit Rome and preach the Gospel there (*1:11-15*).
- Paul's theme is the five parts of salvation:
  ▶ Gospel of Christ.
  ▶ Power of God.
  ▶ Unto salvation.
  ▶ For everyone who believes.
  ▶ By faith.

"For I am not ashamed of the gospel of Christ, for it is the power of God to salvation for everyone who believes, for the Jew first and also for the Greek. For in it the righteousness of God is revealed from faith to faith; as it is written, 'The just shall live by faith'" (*1:16-17*).

Key Word

Gospel: Paul uses the word four times in the opening of Romans (*1:1, 8, 15, 17*). He preaches boldly that the good news of God's work in Christ is for all people who believe. The very nature of good news demands that we proclaim it.

Key Word

Righteousness: This is what God requires to put us in right relationship to Him. God is the source of righteousness. Paul uses this word 35 times in Romans (See *3:5, 5:17, 9:30*).

Key Word

Faith: Even in the Old Testament, righteousness came by belief and trust, not by what we do (See *Hab. 2:4*). Paul uses the word 37 times in Romans. Most often he uses it when talking about righteousness (See *1:17, 4:9, 12:6*).

Key Word

Salvation: Paul uses this word to mean deliverance from sin and its consequences. God rescues us from the power of sin. We are adopted as God's children (See *1:6, 10:10, Joh. 1:12, Eph. 1:5*). Romans deals with the full salvation of the believer from sin's power. Salvation is in three tenses: past, present and future. We need to be saved from:

1. Sin's Pervasiveness. We are *all* unrighteous and our wicked hearts need regeneration (See *Rom. 3:10-18; Jer. 17:9-10; Eph. 2:1-5*).

2. Sin's Penalty (Hell). Through redemption we *have been* saved (See *Rom. 6:23; Rev. 20:14-15, 21:8*).

3. Sin's Power. Through sanctification we *are being* saved and receive new life in Christ (See *Rom. 6; 8:29; 2 Cor. 5:17; Phi. 1:6*).

4. Sin's Presence. Through glorification we *shall be* saved (See *Rom. 8:18-23; Joh. 3:1-3*).

2. All People Are Sinful (*1:18–3:20*)

   A. <u>Gentiles Are Sinful</u> (*1:18-32*)
   Paul begins his argument by showing that even pagans know right from wrong.
- No one has an excuse for not honoring God. Even those who have not heard the Gospel, face judgment (*1:18-20*).

"For since the creation of the world His invisible attributes are clearly seen, being understood by the things that are made, even His eternal power and Godhead, so that they are without excuse" (*1:20*).

- They saw the truth of God in nature and turned away and made their own gods in improper attitudes (*1:21-23*).
  - ▶ They knew God but ignored Him (*1:21*).
  - ▶ Their attitude toward themselves made them into fools (*1:22*).
  - ▶ Their attitude toward the world resulted in wrong use of the body (*1:23*).
- God "*gave them up*"—allowed sin to take its course (*1:24-32*).
  - ▶ Humans chose the lie, and God let them choose.
    - ▷ worshipped created things rather than the Creator (*1:24-25*). God made us in His image but fallen humans seek to make a god in our own image. Every idea or image of God that does not match God's Word is an idol. Every time humans bring God down to a false image, our morality sinks lower as we justify our sin being acceptable to the god we made. This is the heart of idolatry and foolishness.
    - ▷ immorality in sexual behavior (*1:26-27*).
    - ▷ a mind without knowledge of God (*1:28-32*).

"…who, knowing the righteous judgment of God, that those who practice such things are deserving of death, not only do the same but also approve of those who practice them" (*1:32*).

   B. <u>Jews Are Sinful</u> (*2:1–3:8*)
   Paul answers objections the Jews might raise. Being Jewish does not excuse them from judgment.
- Jews know the law of God and still fail (*2:1-4*).
  - ▶ The self-righteous Jew likes to point out the sins of the Gentiles.
  - ▶ The Jews miss the point of God's kindness.

"Or do you despise the riches of His goodness, forbearance, and longsuffering, not knowing that the goodness of God leads to repentance?" (*2:4*)

  - ▶ The Jews believed they would not face judgment because of God's kindness ("goodness") toward them. This was wrong.
  - ▶ God's kindness leads to repentance. It leads back to God. It does not excuse the Jews' sin.

NOTES

NOTES

- The coming judgment is certain (*2:5-11*).
  ▶ "*storing up wrath*" — judgment will come at the end of time.

  "Will render to each one according to his deeds" (*2:6*).

  ▶ Paul shows the difference between eternal life and eternal wrath. Persisting in good works does not earn salvation. Rather, it is proof of true faith (*2:7-8*). (See *Gal. 5:6; Jas. 1:14*).
  ▶ Everyone will face judgment (*2:9-10*).
  ▶ God does not show favorites in judgment. The Jews should not expect special treatment when they sin (*2:11*).
- Standards for judgment (*2:11-16*).

  "For as many as have sinned without law will also perish without law, and as many as have sinned in the law will be judged by the law" (*2:12*).

  ▶ This "law" is the law of Moses. God used the law to reveal Himself to His people.
  ▶ Jews who know the law must obey it to be righteous.
  ▶ God does not expect Gentiles to live by the law of Moses.
  ▶ Yet Gentiles will still please God with some actions. They know the difference between right and wrong.

Christians do not live under the law of Moses. Why should Christians try to understand it?

Key Word
Law: God sets the standard. The law shows us our sin and even makes us want to sin more. Paul uses "law" 73 times in Romans. The most frequent meaning is God's law in the first five books of the Bible, the whole Old Testament or moral conscience. In some places it means a "principle," such as in 3:27 (See also *2:12; 4:13; 7:12; 10:4; 13:8*).

- Jews and judgment (*2:17-28*).
  ▶ The heart matters more than physical circumcision.
  ▶ The Jews claim to be a light for others because they have the law of God. Yet their actions show they do not follow the law God gave them (*2:17-24*).
  ▶ For a man, circumcision is the physical sign of belonging to God. Without obedience, circumcision means nothing (*2:25-27*).

  "… he is a Jew who is one inwardly; and circumcision is that of the heart, in the Spirit, not in the letter; whose praise is not from men but from God" (*2:29*).

- Being a Jew is an inward condition of the heart, not a physical condition. The true sign of belonging to God is the power of the Holy Spirit.
- See *Act. 7:51-54*. Stephen makes this point clearly. He pays with his life. Religious people can get angry at the truth that salvation is by God's grace alone.
- Does the Jew have an advantage? (*3:1-8*).
  Paul answers the question, "If Jews are condemned along with Gentiles, what advantage is there to being a Jew?" (*3:1*).
  - God entrusted His words to the Jews in the Old Testament (*3:2*).
  - Even if some Jews do not have faith, God is still faithful (*3:3-4*; see *Psa. 89:30-37*).
  - Our unrighteousness shows God's righteousness. That is good. But it does not mean we do not deserve judgment for our sin (*3:5-8*).
  - Jews have the words of God, but this does not make them less sinful.

C. <u>All Humans Are Sinful and Condemned</u> (*3:9-20*)
  Paul uses the Old Testament to show the entire human race is guilty before God.
  - Quoting the Jewish Scriptures gives authority to his argument.
    - No one meets God's sinless standard of righteousness (*3:10-12*; see *Psa. 14:1-4; Psa. 53:1-4*).
    - Sin comes from every part of humans (*3:13-14*).
    - Apart from God, humans are inclined to wickedness (*3:15-17*).
    - People without God do not have reverence for God, which is the source of godliness (*3:18*).
  - The whole world stands guilty before God (*3:19-20*).

In your own words, summarize the reasons Paul gives for why everyone will be judged.

"Now we know that whatever the law says, it says to those who are under the law, that every mouth may be stopped, and all the world may become guilty before God" (*3:19*).

- No one will be righteous by keeping the law (*3:20*).
- God did not give the law to provide righteousness. The law leads us to see our sin (*3:20*).

Key Word
Sin: We fall short of the standard God sets. We miss the mark. Sin brings separation from God (See *3:9; 5:12; 7:12; 8:2; 14:23*).

NOTES

3. God Provides Righteousness (*3:21-31*)

Righteousness comes through faith in Jesus Christ, rather than keeping the law. The Old Testament gives evidence of righteousness by faith.

- Everyone falls short of the holy relationship God wants, and "justification" comes to everyone who believes in Jesus by God's grace (*3:21-24*).
    - ▶ "Justified" is a legal term.
    - ▶ Paul uses the Greek word for "justified" 27 times in his letters.
    - ▶ God says the person is "righteous" because of Jesus.
    - ▶ Justification is God's way to bring humans into right relationship with Him. This is true for both Jews and Gentiles.

Key Word
Justification: This means God declares a person to be "not guilty" even though the person deserves to be "guilty." It is a legal word that means "declared righteous" (See *4:25; 5:18*).

- The sacrifice of Jesus shows God's justice (*3:25-26*).
    - ▶ God is righteous, and He also can declare sinners to be righteous. He acts with mercy toward us.

    "…whom God set forth as a propitiation by His blood, through faith, to demonstrate His righteousness, because in His forbearance God had passed over the sins that were previously committed, to demonstrate at the present time His righteousness, that He might be just and the justifier of the one who has faith in Jesus" (*3:25–26*).

    - ▶ Jesus satisfied the justice of God in His death.
    - ▶ God forgave sin in the Old Testament because of His plan to send Jesus as a sacrifice.
    - ▶ Jesus' sacrifice did not take away sins symbolically, as in Old Testament sacrifices (See *Lev. 26*). It took away sins once and for all.
    - ▶ Jesus took the judgment human sin deserves. Those who believe are made righteous because of Jesus.
- Justification comes by faith apart from the law (*3:27-31*).
    - ▶ Paul does not mean we should stop doing good works. He means that works will not make us righteous. No one can boast about good works.
    - ▶ The new principle of righteousness is faith, not law (*3:27*).
    - ▶ Even though Jews have the law, the same principle of faith applies for both Jews and Gentiles.
    - ▶ There is only one God, and He justifies everyone the same way—by faith.

4. "Justification" in the Old Testament (*4:1-25*)

Paul answers the question, "If righteousness comes by faith, why should we keep the law?" This chapter shows that God declares us "not guilty" by God's grace through faith. Abraham, the father of the nation of Israel, is an example of justification by faith.

- We cannot earn justification. This has always been God's way (*4:1-8*). What does the Scripture say? *"Abraham believed God, and it was credited to him as righteousness"* (4:3).
  - ▶ Paul quotes *Gen. 15:6*. God promised Abraham a son. Abraham trusted God to keep His promise. God declared Abraham righteous because he believed.
  - ▶ Abraham did not earn credit for anything. God gave Abraham credit because of his faith (*4:3*).
  - ▶ Abraham's obedience was the fruit of his faith. He obeyed because he believed.

  "Blessed are those whose lawless deeds are forgiven, And whose sins are covered; Blessed is the man to whom the Lord shall not impute sin" (4:7-8).

  - ▶ Paul quotes David (*Psa. 32:1-2*). This is more proof from the Old Testament. Justification by faith has always been God's way.
- Abraham was justified *before* he was circumcised. Therefore justification is not based on physical circumcision (*3:9-12*).
  - ▶ Can the uncircumcised be righteous? Yes. Abraham's example proves it (*3:9-10*).
  - ▶ Circumcision was a sign of Abraham's righteousness. It was not the basis for righteousness (*4:11*).
  - ▶ Abraham is the father of all who believe, whether circumcised or uncircumcised (*4:11*).
- Abraham was justified long *before* the law of Moses. Therefore, justification is not based on the law (*3:13-17*).
  - ▶ In His promise to Abraham, God promised salvation for the world (*3:13*).
  - ▶ Abraham was saved by the Lamb that was slain from the foundation of the world (See Rev. 13:8). Before Abraham lived, Jesus said "I Am" (*Joh. 8:58*). When Abraham wanted to make a sacrifice to God instead of sacrificing his son Isaac, he found a ram *behind* him (*Gen. 22:13*). We are not guilty because of the work Christ did as we look back in faith at His cross.
  - ▶ God's promise to Abraham did not come through the law. Law brings God's wrath, because it points to our sin (*3:13-14*).
  - ▶ God's promises to Abraham were based on faith (*4:16*).
- Abraham was justified by his faith, not his works (*3:18-25*).
  - ▶ God promised a child to Abraham in his old age.
  - ▶ Abraham and Sarah were physically beyond hope of having a child. Paul says Abraham's body was *"as good as dead"* (4:19).
  - ▶ Yet Abraham believed God would keep His promise. He was fully convinced of the power of God (*4:21*).

  "He did not waver at the point of promise of God through unbelief, but was strengthened in faith, giving glory to God, and being fully convinced that what He had promised He was also able to perform" (4:20-21).

NOTES

NOTES

- ▶ Abraham's true faith was counted as righteousness (See *Gen. 15:5-6*).
- ▶ Abraham believed God could bring life from the dead in his body. God justified Abraham because of this faith. God justifies us when we believe *"in him who raised Jesus our Lord from the dead"* (*4:24*).

Explain in your own words how God declares us not guilty.

"... who was delivered up because of our offenses, and was raised because of our justification" (*4:25*).

- ▶ Jesus' Resurrection proves that His sacrifice for us satisfied God's justice.
- ▶ Jesus did for us what we could not do for ourselves.

5. Blessings of Justification (*5:1–11*)

We are blessed with a relationship with God.
- We have peace with God (*5:1*).

"Therefore, having been justified by faith, we have peace with God through our Lord Jesus Christ" (*5:1*).

- ▶ Justification brings a new relationship with God. We are no longer enemies (See *Eph. 2:16; Col. 1:21-22*).
- We have access to God (*5:2*).

Key Word
Grace: God gives us His favor when we do not deserve it. Paul uses this word 22 times in *Romans* (See *1:5; 5:2; 12:3*).

- ▶ In the Old Testament, a heavy curtain in the temple separated the people from God (See *Lev. 16:2*). Jesus removed the curtain and takes us into God's presence.
- We have hope (*5:2-5*).
    - ▶ Joyful hope of the glory of God (*5:2*).
    - ▶ Hope that presents suffering has meaning (*5:3-4*).
    - ▶ Hope that comes with God's love through the Holy Spirit (*5:5*).
- We have assurance of God's grace (*5:6-8*).
    - ▶ God demonstrated His love for us in Christ's death (*5:6-7*).
    - ▶ God loved us when we were not worthy of love (*5:8*).
- We have joyful reconciliation with God (*5:9-11*).

"For if when we were enemies we were reconciled to God through the death of His Son, much more, having been reconciled, we shall be saved by His life" (5:10).

- ▶ We no longer fear God's wrath *(5:9)*.
- ▶ We have the relationship God wants to have with us—no longer enemies; a change of attitude *(5:10)*.
- ▶ Jesus' life continues to bring us life *(5:10-11)*.

6. Sin Came Through Adam. Salvation Came Through Christ *(5:12-21)*

Paul explains sin and grace with illustrations from Adam and Christ.
- The whole human race shares in Adam's sin *(5:12-14)*.
  - ▶ Sin entered the world through Adam and brought physical death as the penalty *(5:12)*.
  - ▶ Everyone begins life with a sinful nature. Sin was in the world even before the law of Moses *(5:13-14)*.
- Sin and death came through one man, Adam. God's grace came through one man, Jesus. Through Christ, God declares us "not guilty" *(5:15-17)*.

"For if by the one man's offence death reigned through the one, much more those who receive abundance of grace and of the gift of righteousness will reign in life through the One, Jesus Christ" (5:17).

- ▶ Christ's work is greater than Adam's sin because it brings God's grace.
- ▶ Condemnation came through Adam. God's grace came through Christ.
- One man's offense brought judgment for all humans. One man's obedience brought life for all humans *(5:18-19)*.
  - ▶ Because Adam was guilty, all humans are guilty *(5:18)*.
  - ▶ *"many"*—This does not mean everyone will be saved, but salvation is available to all *(5:19)*.
  - ▶ *"Made righteous"* is not the same as *"declared righteous"* *(4:3)*. The Holy Spirit continually works to make believers more righteous because God declared them righteous by His grace.
- The law showed sin for what it is *(5:20-21)*.

"As sin reigned in death, even so grace might reign through righteousness to eternal life through Jesus Christ our Lord" (5:21).

- ▶ Sin is never greater than God's grace.
- ▶ Sin reigned in death. Grace reigns in life.
- ▶ The law is a step in between. It shows us our sin. It shows us we need Christ.

Pause at the end of *Romans 5*. Read the chapter again. Paul uses the examples of what happened because of Adam and Christ. On the following page are two columns. Write a summary of what Paul teaches.

NOTES

Adam	*Christ*

7. Old Ways and New Life (*6:1–8:39*)

Paul answers questions about sin and grace.

A. <u>Question: If sin shows God's grace, should we sin more?</u> (*6:1-14*)
   - Paul answers "No! Absolutely not!" He is shocked by the suggestion (*6:1-2*).
   - We died to sin. We are free from the rule of sin (*6:3-4*).

   "Therefore we were buried with Him through baptism into death, that just as Christ was raised from the dead by the glory of the Father, even so we also should walk in newness of life" (*6:4*).

   ▶ Baptism is a picture of being united with Christ (See *Col. 2:12*).
   ▶ The new life of sin is buried. God raises us to new life.
   ▶ In His death and resurrection, Christ conquered sin. Just as Christ was raised from the dead, we live a new life.
   - We are free to live in obedience (*6:5-10*).
     ▶ The *"old self"* was crucified. The believer is no longer the same person (*6:6*).
     ▶ The *"self"* that sin ruled is dead.
     ▶ We are not free of sin, but we are free of sin's power. We have been declared righteous, so sin no longer has a hold on us (*6:7*).
     ▶ Christ died for sin once and for all. Since believers are joined to Christ, they also are alive with Christ (*6:8-10*).
   - We are alive to God (*6:11-14*).

   "Likewise you also, reckon yourselves to be dead indeed to sin, but alive to God in Christ Jesus our Lord" (*6:11*).

   ▶ *"In Christ"*—This is the first time in Romans Paul uses a phrase that appears often in his letters. He stresses the believer's union with Christ. Union with Christ is a reality.

   "Therefore do not let sin reign in your mortal body, that you should obey it in its lusts" (*6:12*).

- The urge to sin is still present in our lives, but sin has no right to be in control. Believers do not have to obey the urge (*6:12, 14*).
- Believers should give themselves, including their bodies, to God. They should not give themselves to sin (*6:13*).
- The law demanded obedience, but we could not obey. Grace gives the power to live as God wants us to live (*6:14*).

B. <u>Question: If we are under grace and not law, are we free to sin?</u> (*6:15–7:6*)
- Paul answers, "No! Absolutely not!" Once again, he is shocked by the suggestion (*6:15*).
- If you offer yourself as a slave, you must obey (*6:16-18*).
  - Being a slave to sin leads to death. Being a slave to obedience, leads to righteousness.

"And having been set free from sin, you became slaves of righteousness" (*6:18*).

  - Paul talks about the Romans, who have obeyed the teaching of the Gospel.
  - Believers have a new master—righteousness. We do not earn justification by being righteous. Rather, righteousness results from God saying that we are not guilty.
- Paul gives a human illustration of slavery (*6:19-23*).
  - Being a slave means being under the control of something.

"But now having been set free from sin, and having become slaves of God, you have your fruit to holiness, and the end, everlasting life" (*6:22*).

  - A slave to sin is not controlled by righteousness. Likewise, a slave to righteousness is not controlled by sin (*6:20*).
  - The two conditions cannot exist together.
  - Being a slave to sin has no benefit. It only leads to death (*6:21*).
  - Being a slave to righteousness leads to holiness and eternal life. A new relationship with God means sin does not need to rule the believer (*6:22*).
- Paul gives an illustration from marriage (*7:1-6*).
  - A law only rules while a person is alive. A woman is married only if her husband is alive. If her husband dies, she is released from that law. Death cancels the relationship (*7:1-3*).
  - Believers have died to the rule of sin. They are released from its power. Death to sin cancels the relationship to the law (*7:4*).

"But now we have been delivered from the law, having died to what we were held by, so that we should serve in the newness of the Spirit and not in the oldness of the letter" (*7:6*).

  - Believers who are released from the rule of sin now live in the Spirit. Only a person who is spiritually alive can bear spiritual fruit (*7:6*; see *Gal. 5:22-23*).

NOTES

NOTES

C. <u>Question: If the law and sin both make slaves, is the law sin?</u> (*7:7-25*)
- Once again, Paul answers, "No! Absolutely not!"
- The law leads to conscience (*7:7-13*).
  ▶ The law shows sin and our need for God. The law is good, but it cannot make us good (*7:7*).
  ▶ The law also stirs up the desire to do what it forbids. Paul uses the example of coveting (*7:8*).
  ▶ Paul was *"alive to God"* before he understood he was guilty under the law. However, he was not conscious of sin until it sprang up like an enemy to kill him (*7:9-11*).

  "For sin, taking occasion by the commandment, deceived me, and by it killed me. Therefore the law is holy, and the commandment holy and just and good" (*7:11-12*).

  ▶ The law of God is not to blame for how human sinful nature responds to the law. The law of God is good (*7:12-13*).
- Paul describes the sinful principle within us (*7:13-25*).
  ▶ We don't always understand what we do, because we do what we hate. Even in sin, God reveals the goodness of the law (*7:14-17*).
  ▶ In our sinful natures we can do nothing good. The sinful nature pulls us away from God (*7:18-20*).
  ▶ Sin wages war within us, even when we seek to please God. On the one hand we are slaves to God. On the other hand our sinful nature is a slave to sin (*7:21-25*).
    ▷ Sin and law are in conflict. The law is not the problem. Sin in us is the problem (*7:21-23a*).
    ▷ The conflict leads to losing hope of being good. Conflict comes before spiritual victory (*7:23b-24*).
    ▷ We keep on fighting sin, but God brings the victory (*7:25*).

D. <u>We Are Free from Condemnation and United with Christ</u> (*8:1-39*)
Paul describes the principle of the Holy Spirit within us.
- The Spirit of Christ empowers us to conquer sinful urges (*8:1-11*).

"There is therefore now no condemnation to those who are in Christ Jesus, who do not walk according to the flesh, but according to the Spirit. For the law of the Spirit of life in Christ Jesus has made me free from the law of sin and death" (*8:1-2*).

  ▶ God did what the law could not do. He condemned sin and did what the law required (*8:1-4*).
  ▶ Paul contrasts life in the sinful nature and life in the Spirit. We cannot fight the sinful nature on our own, but the Spirit of Christ fights and wins (*8:5-10*).
  ▶ The same power that raised Jesus from the dead lives in us (*8:11*).

Key Word
Flesh: Paul uses a word that refers to physical bodies to mean the principle of sin at work in humans; living apart from the Spirit of God. Paul uses the word 25 times in Romans (See *7:18; 8:1; 8:3; 8:9*).

Key Word

Spirit: Paul uses this word 29 times in *Romans. Chapter 8* alone includes 21 times. It can mean human spirit or Holy Spirit. Paul uses the word to show that God's Spirit is at work in us. This is the only way we escape sin's power in us (See *8:1; 8:4; 8:9-11*).

Pause here and read *Romans 8:1-11* **again. In two columns, write the contrasts you see.**

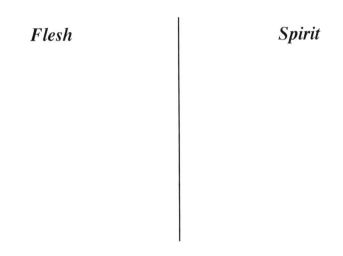

- The Spirit of Christ assures us of our salvation (*8:12-17*).

"For as many as are led by the Spirit of God, these are sons of God. For you did not receive the spirit of bondage again to fear, but you received the Spirit of adoption by whom we cry out, 'Abba, Father'" (8:14-15).

  ▶ We have the Spirit of adoption with an eternal inheritance (*8:14*).
  ▶ We have the Spirit's testimony that we truly are God's children, and no longer slaves to sin (*8:15*).
  ▶ We have the privileges of adoption (*8:14-17a*).
    ▷ *"led by the Spirit of God"* — God guides us (*8:14*).
    ▷ *"sons of God"* — God is our father (*8:15-16*).
    ▷ *"bears witness"* — God's spirit assures us (*8:17*).
    ▷ *"if children, then heirs"* — God gives us an inheritance in heaven (See *1 Pet. 1:4*).
- The Spirit of Christ promises future glory (*8:18-30*).
  ▶ All of creation waits to see the glory of God. God will free the physical world from death and decay (*8:18-20*).
  ▶ We have the *"firstfruits"* of this coming glory. The Holy Spirit is a promise that one day we will have our full inheritance as children of God (*8:22-23*).
  ▶ Our *"hope"* is in the return of Christ. Though we do not see it now, we expect it and wait eagerly. We are sure of what God will do (*8:24-25*).
  ▶ God works in us to make us like Christ (*8:26-30*).
    ▷ Not everything that happens is good. God does not cause everything that happens. This section does not mean God does everything in the way we think is good.

NOTES

▷ *"foreknew," "predestined," "called"* — only God saves by the work of the Holy Spirit (*8:28-29*).
▷ *"work together"* — This word means the parts add up to more than what they are separately.
▷ *"all things"* includes the good (See *Act. 1:8; 2 Cor. 12:9; Eph. 1:17; Col. 4:9; Phi. 3:19; Heb. 13:5*), and the bad (*Jas. 1:2-3; Job 23:10; Psa. 119:67-75; Deu. 8:15-16; Act. 2:21-24*). All things are under God's control.
▷ *"according to His purpose"* — (See *Eph. 1:11*).

"What then shall we say to these things? If God is for us, who can be against us?" (*8:31*).

▶ We still face enemies, but no enemy can defeat God.
▶ God's gift of His Son shows His generosity toward us. Christ died for us. He sits at the right hand of God in power. He intercedes for us. Nothing, not even the law, can condemn us (*8:34*).
▶ Nothing can separate us from the love of God (*8:35-39*).
• Paul lists a full range of possible human physical and spiritual experiences. It is impossible to go beyond God's love.

Key Word
Called: Paul refers to believers as "called" more than any other term (See *1 Cor. 1:2; Gal. 5:14; Eph. 1:18; Col. 3:15; 1 Tim. 6:12; 2 Tim. 1:9*). This is the call of God to salvation to which believers respond positively.

8. Divine Grace and Israel (*9:1–11:36*)

Paul explains the problem of Israel's past and Israel's present. These chapters deal with the nation of Israel, not individuals.

A. <u>Israel's Past: Election, Chosen by God</u> (*9:1-29*)
Paul explains that God has a right to choose and reject as He wants.
• God chose Israel as His people (*9:1-13*).
  ▶ They were adopted as sons. They received the covenants of God. They received the law. They worshiped in the temple. They received God's promises (*9:1-5*).
• God is free to choose. No one can tell God what to do. He did not choose Israel because of good works. This is not a new way for God to act with His people (*9:6-13*).
  ▶ God chose Sarah's son, not Hagar's (*9:8-9*). God chose Isaac and not Esau (*9:10-13*).
  ▶ God chose His people before they could earn the choice. They did nothing to deserve His choosing.
  ▶ It is not love or hate. It is simply a choice.
• We might ask, "If God does what He wishes and does not choose us, how can He blame us?" (*9:14-29*).
  ▶ God acts in line with His character of mercy. He is sovereign. He may choose as He wishes.

"So then it is not of him who wills, nor of him who runs, but of God who shows mercy...Therefore he has mercy on whom He wills, and whom He wills he hardens" (9:16, 18).

- ▸ God is free to show mercy to whom He chooses.
- ▸ The creature cannot tell the Creator what to do. We may not understand what God chooses, but we cannot tell Him what to do (*9:20-21*).
- ▸ The emphasis is on God's nature to be saving and forgiving. His purpose is to show mercy. Paul quotes from the Old Testament to prove his points (See *Hos. 1:10; 2:23; 10:23; Isa. 1:9, 22-23; 13:19; 28:22*).

B. <u>Israel's Present: Rejection</u> (*9:30–10:21*)
Paul explains God rejected the nation of Israel because they tried to be righteous on their own.
- • Israel tried to be righteous by the law. Gentiles became righteous through faith (*9:30-33*).
- • Israel tried to establish their own righteousness. Even though they had God's words, they did not understand God's righteousness (*10:1-4*).
- • True righteousness is near you (*10:5-15*; see *Deu. 30:14; Psa. 119:97-104*).
  - ▸ Paul contrasts two kinds of righteousness: by fulfilling the law (impossible) or by faith (*10:5-8*):

"That if you confess with your mouth, 'Jesus is Lord,' and believe in your heart that God raised Him from the dead, you will be saved. For it is with your heart that you believe and are justified, and it is with your mouth that you confess and are saved" (10:9-10).

- ▸ *"Jesus is Lord"* was the earliest confession of faith.
- ▸ Salvation is for both Jew and Gentile— *"whoever calls on the name of the Lord shall be saved"* (*10:13*; see *Joe. 3:32*).
- ▸ Paul answers natural questions by explaining that God sends someone to preach, the message goes out, people hear, and people believe the message (*10:14-15*; see *Isa. 52:7; Nah. 1:15*).
- • Paul returns to Israel's condition (10:16-21).

"But not all the Israelites accepted the good news. For Isaiah says, 'Lord, who has believed our message?'" (10:16).

- ▸ The good news was available to Israel, but not all believed (*10:16-18*; see also *Isa. 53:1*).
- ▸ Once again, Paul uses Old Testament passages to make his point (*10:18-21*; see *Psa. 19:4; Deu. 32:21; Isa. 65:1-2*).

C. <u>Israel's Future: Salvation</u> (*11:1-36*)
Did God reject His people? Paul answers again, "No. Absolutely not."
- • God's rejection of Israel is not total. Some Israelites have accepted God's grace (*11:1-10*).
  - ▸ Paul himself is an example that some Jews believe (*11:1*).

NOTES

- ▸ *"Reserved for Myself"* — By grace, God has saved a *"remnant"* from Israel (*11:2-6;* see *1 Kin. 19:18*). Elijah thought no one else believed, but he was wrong). The rest are "blinded" because they did not believe.[2]
- ▸ Paul again uses Old Testament passages to make his argument that Israel's indifference to God was a habit (See *Isa. 29:10; Deu. 29:3-4; Psa. 69:22-23*).
- God's rejection of Israel is not final. The rejection brought good to Gentiles as well as Jews (*11:11-24*).
  - ▸ Because Israel stumbled, salvation came to the Gentiles (*11:11-12;* see *Psa. 69:22-23*).
  - ▸ *"Provoke them to jealousy"* — Salvation for the Gentiles wakes up the Jews (*11:11*).
  - ▸ *"Riches for the world"* — If Israel's disobedience brought salvation, how much more will their acceptance of God's righteousness bring life? It will be as if Israel came back from the dead (*11:12-15*).
  - ▸ Gentiles should not boast. They have been grafted into the tree of God's salvation. The salvation of Gentiles depends on the root of the tree — how God has revealed Himself through the Jews (*11:17-24*).
- God saves both Jews and Gentiles by grace (*11:25-32*).
  - ▸ Although Israel is hardened for a time, one day Israel will be saved (*11:25-27;* see *Isa. 59:20-21*).
  - ▸ The Jews are "enemies" because they rejected the Gospel, but they are still God's people (*11:28-30*).
  - ▸ God can still have mercy on the Jews, just as He had mercy on the Gentiles (*11:31-32*).
- Paul praises God for the great plan of salvation, even if we do not understand all of it (*11:33-36;* see *Isa. 40:13; Jer. 23:18; Job 41:11*). Paul praises God for His majesty because God can declare humans "not guilty" by faith.

"Oh, the depth of the riches both of the wisdom and knowledge of God! How unsearchable are His judgments and His ways past finding out!" (*11:33*).

9. Living the Righteous Life (*12:1–15:13*)

A. <u>Transformed Sacrifice</u> (*12:1–8*)
Being declared "not guilty" by God's grace leads to changes in daily living.
- We worship God with our lives.

"I beseech you therefore, brethren, by the mercies of God, that you present your bodies a living sacrifice, holy, acceptable to God, which is your reasonable service. And do not be conformed to this world, but be transformed by the renewing of your mind, that you may prove what is that good and acceptable and perfect will of God" (*12:1-2*).

- ▸ Traits of a sacrifice:
  - ▷ *"living"* — use our bodies to actively serve God.

- ▷ *"holy"* — set apart for God's use.
- ▷ *"acceptable"* — pleasing to God.

NOTES

Name three specific ways people can present themselves as living sacrifices to God.

1.

2.

3.

- A new pattern of living begins not with pride, but with using gifts God gives (*12:3-5*).
  - ▶ Paul uses the illustration of how the human body works as one (*12:3-5*).
  - ▶ The Spirit gives special gifts of grace. Their purpose is not to bring attention to individuals, but to meet the needs of others (See also *1 Cor. 12* and *Eph. 4*).

  "So we, being many, are one body in Christ, and individually members of one another. Having then gifts differing according to the grace that is given us, let us use them…" (*12:5-6*).

B. <u>Transformed Relationships</u> (*12:9-21*)
   The change God makes in us is real. We show it in our relationships.
   - Love takes action (*12:9-10*).
   - Serve eagerly (*12:11-12*).

   "…not lagging in diligence, fervent in spirit, serving the Lord; rejoicing in hope, patient in tribulation, continuing steadfastly in prayer" (*12:11-12*).

   - Practice hospitality. Open your hearts to others (*12:13*).
   - Seek harmony in relationships (*12:14-16*).
   - Stand strong against a world that does not love God (*12:17-21*).
     - ▶ Do not take revenge. Leave that to God (*12:19*).
     - ▶ Live out the power of good (*12:19-20*).
       - ▷ *"heaping coals"* — doing good to one's enemy may lead to his repentance (See also *Deu. 32:35; Pro. 25:21-22*).

   "Do not be overcome by evil, but overcome evil with good" (*12:21*).

C. <u>Righteousness, Love and Duty</u> (*13:1-14*)
   Submission to others — even authority — shows submission to God.

NOTES
- Paul applies teaching on good and evil to secular authorities (*13:1-7*).
  - God establishes civil authorities. When Paul wrote, Nero, an evil emperor, was in power. Still Paul insists believers submit to authority because God establishes them under His authority (*13:1*).
    - *"submit"* — place oneself under another person's authority (*13:1*).
  - Civil authorities and citizens are both accountable to God (*13:2*).
  - God uses governments for His purposes (*13:3-4*).
    Not every government is good. Still, Christians should follow laws as a service to God.
  - Augustine, an early Christian, said, "Government is not necessarily evil but is made necessary because of evil."
    - *Gen. 3:24* is the first mention of a sword in the Bible. This came after sin entered the world. God ruled by force.
    - See *Gen. 9:5-6*. This is the first mention of humans ruling other humans by force.
  - Obedience is a matter of conscience as well as law (*13:5*).[3]
- Love is the superior social way to relate (*13:8-14*).
  - Love makes the law complete. It is the only debt we cannot fully pay (*13:8-10*). To love another person is to fulfill the law.
  - Paul urges love, because the end of the age is coming soon (*13:11-14*).
    - *"sleep"* — a picture of being inactive (See *Eph. 5:14; 1 Pet. 5:8*).
    - *"salvation"* — the return of Christ (See *Rom. 8:23; Heb. 9:28; 1 Pet. 1:5*).

"But put on the Lord Jesus Christ, and make no provision for the flesh, to fulfill its lusts" (13:14).

D. <u>In Relationship with Other Believers</u> (*14:1–15:13*)
Paul speaks to questions of conscience.
- Refrain from judging one another. God will be the judge (*14:1-13*).
  - Perhaps some Jewish Christians did not want to give up dietary laws and other restrictions.
  - We live to please the Lord. Each person should live according to his conscience. Each person will give an account on the Day of Judgment (*14:12*; see also *2 Cor. 5:10; 1 Cor. 3:10-15*).
- Avoid offending one another. Act with love (*14:14-23*).

"Yet if your brother is grieved because of your food, you are no longer walking in love. Do not destroy with your food the one for whom Christ died" (14:15).

  - Each believer has convictions, even Paul. But consideration for others is more important in relationships (See also *1 Cor. 8*).
  - God calls believers to build each other up, not tear each other down (*14:19-20*).
- Stand in unity, whether strong or weak. Christ is our example (*15:1-13*).

"Now may the God of patience and comfort grant you to be like-minded toward one another, according to Christ Jesus, that you may with one

mind and one mouth glorify the God and Father of our Lord Jesus Christ" (*15:5-6*).

- ▶ Follow Christ's example. Think of others. Accept others. Serve others (*15:3, 7, 8*).
- ▶ Paul concludes with a prayer that the Romans will be filled with hope through the power of the Spirit (*15:13*).

How does Paul connect his teaching on salvation with how Christians live? Write down your thoughts.

10. Paul's Personal Plans and Greetings (*15:14–16:27*)

Paul concludes his letter with personal matters.

A. <u>Paul Reviews His Work</u> (*15:14-33*)
   - Paul's past ministry as a minister to the Gentiles (*15:14-16*).
   - Paul's present ministry to preach wherever Christ is not known (*15:17-21*).
   - Paul's future plans for ministry include visiting Rome and Spain (*15:22-33*).
     - ▶ Paul plans to go to Jerusalem to deliver a collection of money for the poor.
     - ▶ Then he plans to travel to Spain. He will stop in Rome on the way.

B. <u>Paul Sends Greetings, Warnings and Blessings</u> (*16:1-27*)
   - Phoebe, who had an official position in the church, likely carried Paul's letter to Rome (*16:1-2*).
   - Paul greets many people he knows in the Roman church. You can feel and sense his relational care for them here (*16:3-16*).
   - Paul warns about divisions in the church (*16:17-19*).
   - Paul relays the greetings of others who are with him (*16:20-24*).
   - Paul gives a final blessing to summarize his message (*16:25-27*).

   "Now unto Him who is able to establish you according to my gospel and the preaching of Jesus Christ, according to the revelation of the mystery kept secret since the world began but now made manifest, and by the prophetic Scriptures made known to all nations, according to the commandment of the everlasting God, for obedience to the faith—to God, alone wise, be glory through Jesus Christ forever. Amen" (*16:25-27*).

NOTES

Suggestions for Preaching From *Romans*

- Explore key concepts for basic teaching on Christian doctrine: grace and law, flesh and Spirit, faith and works, Christ's work of redemption and the Spirit's work of making us holy.

- Explore themes believers experience in daily life: struggles with sin, being sure of salvation by grace through faith, spiritual growth in God's gifts, God's care and sovereignty and living lives of service.

Chapter Two
1 Corinthians

The city of Corinth was located on a narrow piece of land between the Aegean Sea and the Adriatic Sea. Traveling around the southern tip of Greece was dangerous. Instead of sailing around, many ship captains dragged their ships on rollers across the narrow piece of land. Because of this, people in Corinth met travelers from many other cultures. Philosophies and religions mixed freely. The worship of Aphrodite promoted prostitution in the name of religion. The city became famous for immorality.

Paul first arrived in Corinth on his second missionary journey. He worked as a tentmaker with Aquila and Priscilla. On days of Jewish worship, he preached in the synagogue. Silas and Timothy had traveled with Paul before. Now they joined him in Corinth, around AD 52. Paul stayed in Corinth for about a year and a half. *Acts 18:1-18* tells the story of Paul's work in Corinth. After he left Corinth, Paul wrote letters to the church there, and they wrote letters to him.

Paul wrote the book of *1 Corinthians* during his third missionary journey around April-May of AD 56. Probably he had written one letter earlier (see *1 Cor. 5:9*). This letter is a reply to two letters which members of the church wrote to Paul. Their first letter was a report about divisions and immorality in the church. Their second letter was a set of questions. Paul wrote *1 Corinthians* to answer both letters. He was in Ephesus at the time.

What to watch for:

Key words: God's wisdom, idolatry, gifts, resurrection.

Tip: Open your Bible to *1 Corinthians* so you can follow the readings.

1. Conflicts in the Church (*1:1–6:20*)

Paul answers the reports he heard about the church in Corinth.

A. Introduction (*1:1-9*)
   • Paul opens, as usual, with thanks to God for his readers (*1:1-6*).
   • He offers assurance to the church, despite their troubles (*1:7-9*).

B. Divisions in the Church (*1:10–4:21*)
   • The church in Corinth had groups that did not agree with each other (*1:10-17*).
     ▶ Paul received a report about the divisions in the church (*1:11*).
     ▶ People claimed to follow Paul, Apollos, Cephas (Peter) and Christ as if they did not all preach the same Gospel (*1:12*).
     ▶ Paul points to baptism as the sign of union with Christ only. This is the basis of union with each other (*1:13-17*).

NOTES

- Why were believers in Corinth divided? (*1:18–4:5*).
  ▶ They did not understand the Gospel message (*1:18-31*).

  "For Jews request a sign, and Greeks seek after wisdom; but we preach Christ crucified, to the Jews a stumbling block and to the Greeks foolishness, but to those who are called, both Jews and Greeks, Christ the power of God and the wisdom of God" (*1:22-24*).

Why is the phrase *"to those who are called"* important? How does it point out the difference between the first group of Jews and Greeks and the second group of Jews and Greeks? Discuss.

▷ Focus on Christ, not human leaders.
▷ God's wisdom is not the same as human wisdom.
▷ *James 3:13-18* shows the difference between heavenly wisdom (which gives peace) and earthly wisdom (which causes conflict).
▶ *"He who glories, let him glory in the Lord."* God does the work of salvation in the cross of Christ (*1:31*).
▷ God puts us in Christ.
▷ God gives us His wisdom.
▷ God declares us "not guilty" and saves us from the penalty of sin. This is the past tense.
▷ God works in us to make us holy and save us from the power of sin. This is the present tense.
▷ God pays the price of redemption and saves us from the presence of sin. This is the future tense.

Key Word
God's Wisdom: We don't know God through human thought. Christ reveals God to us. We cannot take pride in our own way of thinking. Proverbs tells us of three types of people and their knowledge of God. A "wise or prudent" person knows God's commands and seeks to apply them in life (*Pro. 1:20-33*). A "simple" person lacks the knowledge and understanding of God's commands. This person cannot obey God's Word (*Pro. 22:3; 27:12*). A "foolish" person knows God's commands and chooses to act against them (*Pro. 1:7; 26:16*).

▶ Believers in Corinth did not understand that ministry comes through the power of the Spirit. Faith comes because the Holy Spirit works, not because of human preaching (*2:1-3:23*).
▷ God reveals His wise plan for salvation through the Holy Spirit (*2:1-16*).
▷ True wisdom does not come from human sources (See *Col. 2:7-10*). Sin blinds us (See *Joh. 3:19*) and Satan blinds us (*2 Cor. 4:3-7*).
▷ True wisdom comes from the Spirit of God. It includes "revela-

tion" (the truth God chose to reveal to humans) and "inspiration" (the way God chooses to reveal truth (See *2 Tim. 3:16; 2 Pet. 1:21*).
- ▷ True ministry happens because God is at work, not humans (*3:7, 11*). The Spirit brings understanding of the truth (See *Gal. 6:14*).
- ▷ We may think we have wisdom, but it is nothing apart from God's Spirit at work (*3:18*; see *Pro. 3:7*).
- ▶ They did not understand that human ministers are servants of Christ, unimportant people on their own (*4:1-21*).
- ▷ Some were proud to be rich and important in ministry (*4:8*; see *Rev. 3:17*).
- ▷ True servants of Christ endure hardships with humility. Paul shares his own example (*4:9-13*; see *Act. 18:2; Act. 20:34*).

What conflicts or divisions does your new church in your setting face today?

How does this passage guide you and other Christians who experience conflict?

C. <u>Ignoring Sin Led to Trouble in the Church</u> (*5:1–6:20*)
- The church tolerated incest (*5:1-13*).
  - ▶ *"gathered together...with the power of our Lord Jesus Christ"* — discipline is based on Jesus' authority, not human opinion (*5:4*).
  - ▶ *"that his spirit may be saved"* — The purpose of discipline is to help the man repent (*5:5*; see *1 Tim. 1:20*).
  - ▶ Ignoring the sin could hurt the whole church (*5:11*).
  - ▶ *"Do you not judge those who are inside?"* — Paul is talking about disciplining sin in the church. God judges those outside the church (*5:12*).
- Church members did not solve their own arguments (*6:1-11*).
  - ▶ *"Do you not know...?"* Paul asks this question six times in this chapter. The Corinthians should already know the truths Paul is teaching (*6:2; 6:3; 6:9; 6:15; 6:16*). Not knowing what God's Word teaches hurts the church. It also hurts individual Christians.

"The very fact that you have lawsuits among you means you have been completely defeated already. Why not rather be wronged? Why not rather be cheated? Instead, you yourselves cheat and do wrong, and you do this to your brothers" (*6:7-8*).

NOTES

NOTES

- ▶ Paul reminds his readers God makes believers holy, no matter what their sin, so they should put sinful arguments behind them (*6:9-11*).
- • Church members used Christian freedom to explain their own sexual immorality (*6:12-20*).
  - ▶ The whole person, including the body, is united with Christ (*6:13-14*).
  - ▶ *"Outside the body"* — Corinthians accepted sin by separating body and spirit. Paul says the opposite is true. The body is a *"temple of the Holy Spirit."* (*6:18-19*).

2. Questions in the Church (*7:1–14:40*)

Paul answers questions he received from church members.

A. <u>Questions About Marriage</u> (*7:1-40*)
  - • Question: Is it better to marry or remain unmarried?
    - ▶ If immorality is a temptation, it is better to marry. Also, husbands and wives should not deprive each other (*7:2-5*).
    - ▶ Paul has a personal opinion, but it is not a command from God (*7:6-9*).
  - • Question: What about divorce?
    - ▶ *"A wife must not separate"* — a believing husband and wife should not leave each other. This is a command from the Lord, not Paul (*7:10-11*).
    - ▶ Paul writes about an unbeliever married to a believer, but this is not a command from the Lord. Believers should remain married unless the spouse who does not believe chooses to leave (*7:12-16*).
    - ▶ Believers should be faithful to Christ, whether married or unmarried when they come to faith (*7:17-24*).

    "Let each one remain in the same calling in which he was called (7:20)…Brethren, let each one remain with God in that state in which he was called" (*7:24*).

  - • Question: Can marriage and ministry work together?
    - ▶ Paul again gives his own opinion, not the Lord's command (*7:25*).
    - ▶ Paul saw troubled times ahead. It would be easier *not* to be married (*7:26-28*).
    - ▶ Married people should remain dedicated to God's work. Do not let marriage make this present life more important than service to God (*7:29-39*; see *2 Cor. 6:11-18*; the balance of marriage and ministry is one reason why Paul warns against being unequally yoked with unbelievers).
  - • Question: How long does the marriage vow last?
    - ▶ *"As long as her husband lives"* — The death of a spouse frees the other person to marry again. The new spouse should be a believer (*7:39*).
    - ▶ *"I also have the Spirit of God"* — Even in his own opinion, Paul believes God guides what he writes (*7:40*).

B. Questions About Worship (*8:1–11:1*)
- Question: Can believers eat meat that was sacrificed to idols?
  - ▶ Some meat left over from pagan sacrifice was sold in the market. Some Christians felt it was wrong to eat this meat.
  - ▶ *"An idol is nothing"* — An idol has no power, so the meat is simply meat (*8:4, 8*; see *Isa. 41:24; Deu. 4:35, 39*).
  - ▶ However, do not use this freedom to offend another believer's conscience (*8:9-13*).

  "But beware lest somehow this liberty of yours become a stumbling block to those who are weak...Therefore, if food makes my brother stumble, I will never again eat meat, lest I make my brother stumble" (*8:9, 13*).

- Question: Is Paul really an apostle?
  - ▶ Some in Corinth questioned Paul's authority. He defends his apostleship. He saw Jesus on the road to Damascus (*Act. 9*), and the church in Corinth was a result of Paul's work (*9:1-2*).
  - ▶ *"But we have not used this right"* — Paul had a right to many things that he did not claim. He put his ministry for Christ above his personal wishes (*9:3-23*).

  "For though I am free from all men, I have made myself a servant to all, that I might win the more...Now this I do for the gospel's sake, that I may be a partaker of it with you" (*9:19, 23*).

  - ▶ *"Receives the prize"* — a reward for endurance, not earning salvation (*9:24-27*; see *Phi. 1:29; 2 Tim. 2:12*).
- Question: Are pagan sacrifices dangerous?
  - ▶ Paul uses Israel's history as a warning about using freedom the wrong way.
  - ▶ God disciplined the Israelites when they shared in idol worship and immorality. This is a reminder not to test the Lord. Christian freedom does not excuse sin (*10:1-11*).
  - ▶ *"Ends of the ages has come"* — God's plans are coming to fulfillment.
  - ▶ With God's help, we can stand firm when tempted to sin (*10:12-13*).

  "No temptation has overtaken you except such as is common to man; but God is faithful, who will not allow you to be tempted beyond what you are able, but with the temptation will also make the way of escape, that you may be able to bear it" (*10:13-14*).

  - ▶ Idols were everywhere in Greek culture. If Christians participate in pagan worship, they violate their union with Christ (*10:14–11:1*).
- Feasts honoring idols and the Lord's Supper cannot go together (*10:14-22*).
- *"All things are lawful"* — the basis of Christian freedom. However, we should not use freedom to cause someone else to go against conscience (*10:23–11:1*).

NOTES

Key word

Idolatry: worship of something humans have made, rather than God, who created all things. Also, anything that is put in the place of God is idolatry. Even though idols are not true gods, idolatry is dangerous. While Paul says eating meat sacrificed to idols is not sinful, worshiping idols is.

    C. <u>Christian Worship</u> (*11:2–34*)
- Show respect in public worship (*11:2-16*).
  - ▶ *"Head"* — Christ has authority over every man, and a husband has authority over his wife. Christ is not inferior to God, and women are not inferior to men (*11:3*; see *Eph. 1:22; 4:15; 5:23*).
  - ▶ Both women and men prayed and prophesied (*11:4-5*). Paul was concerned that worship honor God. In first century culture, it was a disgrace for a woman's head to be uncovered in public.[4]
  - ▶ *"Does not even nature itself teach"* — Paul finds it natural for men and women to be different. However, men and women are not independent of the other (*11:11-15;* see *Gal. 3:28*).

  "Nevertheless, neither is man independent of woman, nor woman independent of man, in the Lord" (*11:11*).

  - ▶ All the churches observed head covering customs. Corinth should also follow this practice (*11:16*).
- The Lord's Supper (*11:17-24*).
  - ▶ *"Divisions"* — may refer to church members from different classes of society. Church members were not coming together as equal. However, divisions showed who was being faithful (*11:17-19*).[5]
  - ▶ Early Christians shared a *"love"* feast with the Lord's Supper (See *2 Pet. 2:13; Jude 12*). However, some church members turned it into a time of selfishness (*11:20-22*).
  - ▶ Paul reminds the Corinthians of how the Lord's Supper began. He asks them to examine their practices (*11:23-33*).

  "Therefore, whoever eats the bread or drinks the cup of the Lord in an unworthy manner will be guilty of the body and blood of the Lord" (*11:27*).

    D. <u>Spiritual Gifts</u> (*12:1–14:40*)
- The Spirit gives spiritual gifts (*12:1-11*).
  - ▶ Paul answers another question the Corinthians asked. He does not want them to be ignorant, as unbelievers are (*12:1-3*).

  "But the manifestation of the Spirit is given to each one for the profit of all…But one and the same Spirit works all these things, distributing to each one individually as He wills" (*12:7-11*).

  - ▶ *"Each one"* — Each believer receives gifts (*12:4*).
  - ▶ *"For the profit of all"* — One Holy Spirit gives gifts to believers. The gifts are different, but all gifts are to build up the church, not individuals (*12:4-11*).

- ▷ *"Word of wisdom"* — ability to express the Gospel message with insight into God's truth.
- ▷ *"Word of knowledge"* — ability to apply God's truth to life situations.
- ▷ *"Faith"* — ability to believe God for great things.
- ▷ *"Gifts of healing"* and *"workings of miracles"* — physical demonstrations of God's power at work.
- ▷ *"Prophecy"* — telling the truth of God to His people.
- ▷ *"Discerning of spirits"* — special ability to know the difference between the works of God and demonic work, or between the truth of God and the teaching of His Word and false teaching.
- ▷ *"Tongues"* — speaking languages one has not studied.
- ▷ *"Interpretation of tongues"* — explain or translate tongues/languages.

- Christians have different gifts, but the same Spirit baptizes them all (*12:12-31*). The Corinthians had conflict and divisions based on selfishness. Paul points them back to unity that comes from thinking of the whole church.
  - ▶ Paul illustrates by describing the human body. The body has many different parts, and each one is important (*12:12-26*).
    - ▷ The Spirit's baptism brings unity, not division.
    - ▷ God gives His Holy Spirit to all believers. No one has new life any other way. This binds all believers together.
  - ▶ In the same way, the church is the body of Christ. The body of Christ has different parts, and each one is important (*12:27-30*).
    - ▷ *"Apostles"* and *"prophets"* — the foundation of the church (See *Mat. 16:18; Eph. 2:20*). Jesus chose apostles to be with Him in His years of ministry on earth. They also witnessed the resurrection (*Act. 1:21-22*).
      - ◆ Some commentators interpret the word to a wider meaning of "missionary" (See *2 Cor. 11:5; Rom. 16:7*).
    - ▷ *"Teachers"* — perhaps linked to pastoral work, certainly systematic in presentation of the Word.
    - ▷ Apostles, prophets and teachers ministered to the whole church.
    - ▷ *"Gifts of administration"* — abilities to organize and lead the ministries of the church.
  - ▶ *"Best gifts"* — The Corinthians may have been trying to say some gifts were more important than others. That would mean some people were more important than others. Paul introduces the "most excellent" way to use gifts. Having certain gifts is not as important as using gifts the right way to build up the whole church (*12:31*).

NOTES

Key Word

Gifts: The Holy Spirit gives gifts of grace to believers. Each believer receives gifts. Each believer is called to use the gifts for the good of everyone, not for individual pride. Paul teaches on gifts in *1 Cor. 12:8-10; Eph. 4:7-11* and *Rom. 12:3-8*. The lists are not the same every time, but each time Paul stresses the unity that gifts bring to the body.

NOTES

What do you find most confusing about spiritual gifts?

What are your particular spiritual gifts when you look at all the various listings above?

What does *1 Corinthians 12* say that helps you better understand spiritual gifts for your new church?

- Without love, gifts mean nothing (*13:1-13*).

    "Though I speak with the tongues of men and of angels, but have not love, I have become sounding brass or a clanging cymbal. And though I have the gift of prophecy, and understand all mysteries and all knowledge, and though I have all faith, so that I could move mountains, but have not love, I am nothing" (*13:1-2*).

    ▶ Paul describes the positive traits of love and the traits that are not part of real love (*13:4-8*).
    ▶ *"Now I know in part," "now we see but a poor reflection"* — Nothing else ever replaces love. The gifts from *1 Cor. 12* will fade away, but love is permanent (*13:8-13*).
- Use the gifts to build up the body (*14:1-25*).
    ▶ *"Tongues"* and *"Prophecy"* — In public worship, the church cannot understand someone who speaks in tongues, but prophecy (a message to believers from the Holy Spirit) is in plain language (*14:1-12*).
    ▶ Tongues may be used in worship if someone can interpret.
    ▶ For the church body, it is better if everyone can understand (*14:13-25*).
- Worship should be orderly (*14:26-40*).
    ▶ *"Each of you... anyone"* — Everyone in the church could share in worship (*14:26-29*).[6]
    ▶ *"Let your women keep silent"* — Paul already said that women may

pray and prophesy in public (*11:5*). Some women may have become disorderly in the way they took part in worship (*14:33-39*). Archaeological reliefs found in both Corinth and Ephesus support this.

Based on *1 Corinthians 11–14*, what principles should guide Christian worship? Discuss.

E. <u>The Resurrection of Christ and Christians</u> (*15:11-58*)
- Christ's Resurrection is central to the Gospel Paul preached (*15:1-11*).
- Some in Corinth doubted any resurrection at all (*15:12-34*).
    - ▶ If there is no resurrection, then even Christ was not raised (*15:12-13*).
    - ▶ If Christ was not raised, preaching is useless (*15:14, 16*), and eyewitnesses would be liars (*15:15*), and faith is pointless (*15:17*), and the dead have been destroyed (*15:18*).
    - ▶ *"Firstfruits"* — Christ has been raised.
        - ▷ Firstfruits are the part of the harvest that comes first. Paul uses images from the Old Testament. God's people gave the first part of the harvest to the Lord (See *Lev. 23:10-11, 17, 20*). This was a promise that the rest of the harvest would come.
        - ▷ As "firstfruits," Christ's resurrection points to the resurrection of all believers (*15:19-20;* see *Rev. 20:1-6*).

        "But Christ has indeed been raised from the dead, the firstfruits of those who have fallen asleep" (*15:20*).

    - ▶ *"By man came death"* — Death came through Adam. Life comes through Christ (*15:21-22;* see *Rom. 5:12-19*).
    - ▶ *"The end"* — the second coming of Christ and events that come with it. The kingdom of God triumphs even over death (*15:24-28*).
    - ▶ Paul lived with risks every day. Without resurrection, dangers would have no meaning (15:29-34).
        - ▷ *"baptized for the dead"* — The New Testament church did not follow this practice, and the apostle Paul did not teach it.
        - ▷ *"for"* — this phrase should be translated "for the hope of the dead." The hope of the dead is resurrection. Baptism of the believer is a picture of the believer's death, burial and resurrection in Christ.
        - ▷ Marcion introduced the practice of baptism on behalf of the dead to Christians about AD 150 as part of his own religion.
        - ▷ The Mormons teach this false doctrine by misusing this verse. The practice of being baptized for those who have died is based upon a wrong understanding of *1 Cor. 15:29*.

NOTES

Key Word

Resurrection: In the Resurrection, God raised Jesus Christ physically from the dead. He appeared to hundreds of people after He rose. The Resurrection is an event of history, not only a spiritual concept. Because Jesus was raised, believers look forward to physical resurrection as well.

According to Paul, what would happen to the Christian faith without the Resurrection?

- Christians will have resurrection bodies (*15:35-58*)
    - *"Foolish"* — The Resurrection may be hard to understand. This does not mean it is not true (*15:25–37*).
    - Paul gives examples from nature. God created great variety. He can certainly raise the dead with a new body (*15:38-41*).
    - The earthly body is weak and sinful. The resurrection body is permanent and glorious (*15:42-44*).
    - Paul contrasts the natural body and the spiritual body. The natural body dies. The spiritual body will never die. Adam gave humans a natural body. Christ will give a spiritual body that is real (*15:44-49*).

    "Now this I say, brethren, that flesh and blood cannot inherit the kingdom of God; nor does corruption inherit incorruption. Behold, I tell you a mystery: We shall not all sleep, but we shall all be changed" (*15:50-51*)

    - *"Trumpet," "in the twinkling of an eye"* — resurrection will happen in an instant (*15:52-54;* see *1 The. 4:13-18*).
    - Resurrection swallows up death. Believers have final victory over sin (*15:55-58*).

3. Requests and Greetings (*16:1-24*)

A. <u>Collection for Jerusalem</u> (*16:1-4*)
- On Paul's third missionary journey, he collected money to give to Christians in Jerusalem who were in need.
- Christians in Jerusalem may have suffered from famine or persecution (See *Act. 8:1; 11:28*).

B. <u>Personal Requests</u> (*16:5-18*)
- Paul hopes to visit Corinth soon (*16:5-9*).
- Paul asks the Corinthians to care for Timothy (*15:10-11;* see *Act. 19:22*).
- Paul closes with personal requests and encouragements (*16:12-24*).

Suggestions for Preaching From *1 Corinthians*

- Explore themes of relationships in the church: Christian response to immorality, freedom in Christ, sincere Christian worship, and what the Resurrection means for the Christian.

- Examine the theme of the Cross: what the Cross means to relationships, the meaning of the Lord's Supper, the supreme gift of love because of the Cross, and how the Cross leads believers to the future.

- Study God's purpose for the Christian life in gifts and godly living.

- Identify guidelines for making choices in sensitive situations.

Chapter Three
2 Corinthians

Paul's correspondence with the church in Corinth continued after he wrote *1 Corinthians*. Sometime fairly soon, Paul made a visit to Corinth. He describes the visit as "painful" (*2 Cor. 2:1*). After the visit, he wrote a "sorrowful letter" (*2 Cor. 2:4; 7:8*) that has been lost. This lost letter commanded church discipline of a person who led people against Paul. Paul sent the letter with Titus. Paul left Ephesus and went to Troas to wait for Titus to bring a report. Titus gave a good report of the progress of Christians in Corinth. Paul wrote *2 Corinthians* around September-October of AD 56 to express his joy that problems were better. He also defended his authority as an apostle.

What to watch for:

Key words: reconciliation, new covenant, suffering.

Tip: Open your Bible to *2 Corinthians* so you can follow the readings.

1. Greetings and Thanksgiving (*1:1-11*)

  A. Traditional Opening
   - Paul's usual opening of thanks focuses on comfort in suffering.
   - *"Tribulation"* — God comforts us in our troubles with the result that we can comfort others (*1:4-7*).

  B. Paul Shares His Sufferings (*1:8-11;* see also *Act. 19:23-41* and *1 Cor. 15:31-32*).

2. Motives for Ministry (*1:12–7:16*)

  A. Paul Explains His Motives and Plans (1:12–2:11)
   - Paul explains why he visited Corinth (1:12–2:5).
     ▶ Some accused Paul of not being sincere, but he has a clear conscience (*1:12–13*).
     ▶ Paul was accused of not keeping his word, but he has been faithful to God. God keeps His word (*1:14-20*).
     ▶ Paul's call comes from God (*1:21-24*).

     "Now He who establishes us with you in Christ and has anointed us is God, who also has sealed us and given us the Spirit in our hearts as a guarantee" (*1:21-22*).

      ▷ *"anointed"* — empowered by God.
      ▷ *"sealed us"* — The Spirit is a guarantee of belonging to God.
     ▶ Paul made one painful visit to Corinth. He does not want to come again in sorrow. He wants to come in joy (*2:1-5*).

NOTES
- Paul instructs forgiveness (*2:6-11*).
  ▶ *"If anyone has caused grief"* — This may refer to the man in *1 Cor. 5* or someone who sinned against Paul during the painful visit (*2:5*).
  ▶ *"Punishment"* — Church discipline led to repentance. Now the church may show love and forgiveness. The goal of discipline is repentance and restoration of the sinner (*2:6-11;* see *Gal. 6:1-2*).

B. <u>Paul's Ministry of the Gospel</u> (*2:12–6:10*)
- Triumph in ministry (*2:12-17*).

"But thanks be to God who always leads us in triumph in Christ, and through us diffuses the fragrance of His knowledge in every place" (*2:14*).

  ▶ Paul uses a metaphor of the Roman triumphal procession for a victorious general.[7]
  ▶ The Gospel gives life (victory) to those who receive it. To others, it is the smell of death (*2:15-16*).
  ▶ *"Peddling"* — Some people used religion to make a profit. Paul's motives for ministry are pure (*2:17*).
- Recommendation for ministry (*3:1-5*).
  ▶ Paul needs no letter to recommend him for ministry. The Corinthians themselves are his letter (*3:1-3*).
  ▶ Qualification for ministry comes by the Spirit of God (*3:4-5*).
    ▷ *"such trust"* — Paul is sure God would make his ministry effective through Christ (*3:4*).
- Privilege of the ministry (3:7-18).
  Paul names differences between the Old Testament ministry and New Testament ministry.
  ▶ *"Engraved on stone,"* ministry of the Spirit is *"even more glorious"* (*3:7-8;* see *Rom. 7:10; Exo. 34:1*).
    ▷ The law given through Moses would pass away.
    ▷ The Spirit gives eternal life.
  ▶ *"Ministry of condemnation," "ministry that brings righteousness"* (*3:9-10*).

"If the ministry of condemnation had glory, the ministry of righteousness exceeds much more in glory. For even what was made glorious had no glory in this respect, because of the glory that excels" (*3:9-10*).

  ▷ The law was good, but no one can be righteous under the law.
  ▷ By grace, God declares anyone who believes "not guilty." (See *Rom. 3:21-24*).

Discuss the differences between the two ministries Paul describes. Why is the difference important?

- Honesty in the ministry (*4:1-6*).
  - ▶ *"Manifestation of the truth"* — No matter how difficult ministry was, Paul speaks boldly (*4:1-3*).
  - ▶ *"God of this age has blinded"* — Satan hides the truth. Paul preaches plainly (*4:4-5*). (See *Joh. 12:31; Joh. 12:40;* we need to be compassionate and patient with unbelievers, *2 Tim. 2:24*).

  "For it is the God who commanded light to shine out of darkness, who has shone in our hearts to give the light of the knowledge of the glory of God in the face of Jesus Christ" (*4:6*).

  - ▶ God is the original Creator. Now He makes a new creation (*4:6*).
- Ministry brings troubles (*4:7-15*).
  - ▶ *"Treasure," "earthen vessels"* — In the first century, people hid valuable items in common clay pots.
  - ▶ The Gospel is a treasure hidden in frail humans.
  - ▶ Ministry brings troubles, but troubles do not destroy us (*4:7-10*).

  "For we who live are always delivered to death for Jesus' sake, that the life of Jesus also may be manifested in our mortal flesh" (*4:11*).

  - ▷ Our suffering is a way of sharing in Christ's suffering.
  - ▷ Because Paul was willing to suffer, others heard the Good News.
- Ministry may be discouraging, but we have confidence in God (*4:16–5:10*).
  - ▶ *"Renewed day by day"* — The Gospel overflows even in hard times (*4:16*).
  - ▶ *"Light affliction"* — From an eternal perspective, our troubles are small (*4:17-18*).

NOTES

Name three ways Paul's words in *2 Corinthians 4* can encourage believers who suffer.

1.

2.

3.

NOTES

- Our bodies will die. God will give us resurrection bodies (*5:1-10*).
  - When we suffer, we long for our future in heaven. The Holy Spirit is a guarantee of the future (*5:1-5*).

  "Now He who has prepared us for this very thing is God, who also has given us the Spirit as a guarantee. So we are always confident, knowing that while we are at home in the body we are absent from the Lord. For we walk by faith, not by sight" (*5:6-7*).

  - We are confident of our future in heaven after death (*5:6-10;* see also *Phi. 1:23; Luk. 23:43*).
  - 2 Cor. 5:10 speaks of the judgment seat of Christ. After they are resurrected, believers must stand before Christ and give an account of how they lived after they became Christians. This includes motives as well as actions.
- The love of Christ motivates ministry (*5:11-21*).
  - *"Fear the Lord"* — We will one day give an account to God. This is reason to preach the Gospel (*5:11;* see *Rom. 2:16; Rom. 14:10-12; Eph. 6:8*).
  - The love of Christ is a reason to preach the Gospel (*5:12-15*).

  "For the love of Christ compels us, because we judge thus: that if One died for all, then all died; and He died for all, that those who live should live no longer for themselves, but for Him who died for them and rose again" (*5:14-15*).

  - The Gospel transforms hearts. This is reason to preach. We share Christ's *"ministry of reconciliation"* (*5:18-20*).

Key Word
Reconciliation: to put an end to opposition; change from being enemies to peace. Because of Christ's death and resurrection, we are no longer enemies of God. God does this work, not us (See also *Rom. 5:1-10*). Believers share in the ministry of reconciliation when they share the Gospel with others.

- Ministry is for God, not for ourselves (*6:1-10*).
  - Paul lists the traits of true servant ministry.
  - This compares with false teachers who wanted to be important.

C. <u>Paul Asks the Corinthians to Respond to His Message</u> (6:11–7:4)
  - Paul has been honest. He asks the readers to open their hearts to him (*6:11-13*).
  - Paul asks the Corinthians to separate from false teaching (*6:14-7:1*).
    - *"Do not be yoked together"* (*6:14;* see *Deu. 22:10*). God told Israel not to yoke a clean animal (ox) with an unclean animal (donkey).
    - The church in Corinth had a history of joining groups that worshiped idols or followed false leaders (See *2 Cor. 11:13-14*).
    - Paul reminds the Corinthians of their true relationship to God. He urges them to separate from things that take them away from God (*6:14–7:1*).

"And what accord has Christ with Belial? Or what part has a believer with an unbeliever? And what agreement has the temple of God with idols? For you are the temple of the living God" (6:15-16).

    ▷ This does not mean to have nothing to do with unbelievers.
    ▷ It means not to participate in the sinful ways of unbelievers.
- Paul asks again for readers to open their hearts *(7:2-4)*.

How can Christians separate from false teaching but still connect with people in their culture?

What is your plan to reach your community for Christ and yet stay true to the Word of God?

  D. <u>Comfort from Sorrow</u> *(7:5-16)*
    - The believers obeyed Paul *(7:5-12)*.
      ▶ Titus gave a good report to Paul about Corinth *(7:5-7)*.
      ▶ Paul's "painful letter" caused sorrow, but it also led to repentance *(7:8-11)*.

"For godly sorrow produces repentance leading to salvation, not to be regretted…What diligence it produced in you" (7:10-11).

        ▷ We do not have Paul's "painful letter" in the New Testament.
        ▷ Although it was hard to write a "painful letter," speaking honestly and with love resulted in change.
    - The believers showed love when they received Titus *(7:13-16)*.

3. Paul Asks for Generosity for Believers in Jerusalem *(8:1–9:15)*

  A. <u>Paul Gives an Update on the Collection</u> *(8:1-24)*
    - Paul tells of the generosity of churches in Macedonia *(8:1-5)*.
      ▶ *"Churches of Macedonia"* — This is the northern part of present-day Greece. Paul started churches there in Philippi, Thessalonica and Berea *(8:1)*.

"That in a great trial of affliction the abundance of their joy and their deep poverty abounded in the riches of their liberality. For I bear wit-

NOTES

ness that according to their ability, yes, and beyond their ability, they were freely willing" (8:2-3).

- ▶ Macedonians gave generously. They believed giving was a special favor to them (8:2-5).
- Paul urges the church in Corinth to be generous as well (*8:6-15*).
  - ▶ *"In faith"* — Believers in Corinth had many gifts, including the gift of faith (8:6-7).
  - ▶ *"Grace of our Lord"* — Jesus is the example for giving (8:8-9).

"For you know the grace of our Lord Jesus Christ, that though He was rich, yet for your sakes He became poor, that you through His poverty might become rich" (8:9).

  - ▷ Jesus gave up heavenly riches to come to earth (See *Phi. 2:7-8*).
  - ▷ *"you...might become rich"* — Jesus gives spiritual riches to those who believe (8:9).
  - ▶ *"Complete the doing of it"* — The Corinthians had started a collection. Now it was time to finish (*8:10-12*).
  - ▶ *"Equality"* — Paul's goal is not to cause hardship for the Corinthians. Believers everywhere can share what they have (*8:13-15*).

In your own words, write what you think is Paul's main point about generosity.

- Paul sends Titus for the collection (*8:16-24*).
  - ▶ *"Chosen by the churches"* — After collecting money in Corinth, Titus will go with Paul to Jerusalem (*8:16-21*).
  - ▶ *"Fellow worker concerning you"* — Titus earned trust in Corinth (*8:22-24*).

B. Reasons for Generosity (*9:1-15*)
  - The Corinthians were ready to give to the collection (*8:1-5*).
    - ▶ Paul bragged about them. Their eagerness inspired other churches (8:2).
    - ▶ Now they need help with their good intentions (*8:3-5*).

"Yet I have sent the brethren, lest our boasting of you should be in vain in this respect, that, as I said, you may be ready" (9:3).

  - ▷ *"ashamed of this confident boasting"* — Paul planned to visit. Some Macedonians would come with him. They would know if the Corinthians finished the job.[8]
  - Generous giving enriches the giver (*9:6-11*).

- ▶ *"Sowing"* and *"reaping"* — In this picture of nature's harvest, each person can choose how much to plant (*9:6; see also Pro. 11:24-25; 19:17; Luk. 6:38; Gal. 6:7*).
- ▶ Each person decides privately what to give cheerfully (*9:7*).
- ▶ *"Supply and multiply the seed"* — God provides for those who give so they may continue to give (*9:8-11*).
- Giving is an offering of thanks to God (*9:12-15*).

"This service that you perform is not only supplying the needs of God's people but is also overflowing in many expressions of thanks to God" (*9:12*).

- ▶ *"They glorify God for your obedience"* — Giving brings glory to God (*9:12-13*).
- ▶ *"Indescribable gift"* — What we give to God can never compare to what God gives to us in Jesus (*9:14-15*).

4. Paul Defends His Ministry (*10:1-13:10*)

Paul speaks to the few people in Corinth who still oppose him.

A. Paul's Position as an Apostle (*10:1–12:18*)
   - Paul's critics doubt his authority (*10:1-18*).
     - ▶ *"Lowly," "bold"* — Critics accuse Paul of being strong in his letters, but weak in person (*10:1-2; see also 10:10*).
     - ▶ Paul does not seek the world's standard (*10:3-6*).

     "Casting down argument and every high thing that exalts itself against the knowledge of God, bringing every thought into captivity to the obedience of Christ" (*10:5*).

     - ▶ *"Authority, which the Lord gave us for edification"* — Paul's purpose is not to tear down, but to build up with authority (*10:7-11*).
     - ▶ *"Limits of the sphere which God has appointed us"* — False teachers boast that they are the highest standard. Paul's focus is on the job God gave him to do (*10:12-18*).
   - Paul explains his policy about money (*11:1-15*).
     - ▶ He guards against the false teachers who lead the Corinthians astray. He points out some have been too quick to believe false teachers (*11:1-6*).

     "For if he who comes preaches another Jesus whom we have not preached, or if you receive a different spirit which you have not received, or a different gospel which you have not accepted-you may as well put up with it!" (*11:4-5*).

     - ▶ Paul preaches without charging money (*11:7-12*).
       - ▷ In Paul's day, professional teachers charged money. Some churches supported Paul (*11:7-10*).

NOTES

- ▷ *"cut off the opportunity"* — Paul did not take money from the Corinthians because he did not want other teachers to think they were on the same level with him (*11:11-12*).
- ▷ *"false apostles"* — Paul's critics called themselves apostles of Christ.
- ▶ Paul exposes false apostles (*11:13-15*).
- Paul boasts about service (*11:16-33*).
  - ▶ Paul boasts to show that his ministry is strong. Critics accused him of being weak, while others were wise (11:16-21).

"What I speak, I speak not according to the Lord, but as it were, foolishly, in this confidence of boasting. Seeing that many boast according to the flesh, I will also boast. For you put up with fools gladly, since you yourselves are wise!" (*11:17-19*).

- ▶ Paul boasts about his background (*11:21-33*).
  - ▷ His heritage is spotless (*11:21-22*).
  - ▷ His sufferings prove his ministry (*11:23-29*).
  - ▷ He even boasts in weakness (*11:30-33*).
- Paul's boast about visions (*12:1-10*).
  - ▶ *"Man in Christ"* — Paul is modest. He is talking about himself (*12:2*).
  - ▶ *"Third heaven," "Paradise"* — People in Paul's time often spoke of three heavens. The first heaven is where birds fly. The second heaven is where the sun, moon and stars are. The third heaven is where God lives (*12:2, 4*).
  - ▶ *"Thorn in my flesh"* — Paul does not explain what this is. It might be: a physical ailment; a temptation; persecution (*12:7-19*).[9]
  - ▶ Weakness in us points to Christ's power at work.

"Therefore most gladly I will rather boast in my infirmities, that the power of Christ may rest upon me" (*12:9*).

B. <u>Paul's Concern for the Corinthians</u> (*12:11–13:10*)
  - Paul boasts because the Corinthians listened to false apostles (*12:11-18*).
    - ▶ The serious situation means that Paul must boast to bring them back to the truth.
    - ▶ *"Signs," "wonders and mighty deeds"* — Paul did these things in Corinth. These things prove his authority (*12:11-13*).
      - ▷ These are supernatural acts.
      - ▷ Miracles proved the message (signs), stirred up awe in the people who saw them (wonder), and showed God's power (mighty deeds).
    - ▶ *"Third time"* — Paul will visit Corinth a third time. He is ready to sacrifice for them (*12:14-18*).
      - ▷ *"crafty," "cunning"* — Paul is being sarcastic, as if he tricked them into not giving him money.
  - Paul's aim is to build up the Corinthians (*12:19–13:10*).
    - ▶ He fears he will find divisions among them again (*12:19-21*).
    - ▶ Paul is not afraid to be firm if he finds sin in Corinth (*13:1-4*).

- ▶ Believers should look at their own hearts (*13:5-10*).
  - ▷ Believers asked Paul to prove himself to them. Now they must prove themselves (*13:5-8*).
  - ▷ *"perfection"* — Paul prays for healing of divisions in the church (*13:9-10*).

5. Personal Greetings, Encouragement, Benediction (*13:11-14*)

Suggestions for Preaching From *2 Corinthians*

- Look at themes of hope and comfort in times of trials.

- Teach on how to recognize solid doctrine and act in love if false teaching happens.

- Find lessons on generosity and the connections between congregations.

Chapter Four
GALATIANS

Who were the Galatians? When did Paul write the letter to the Galatians? These two questions are connected. In the first century, "Galatia" could mean an area of Asia Minor, to the north. Or, it could mean a group of cities to the south.

On his first missionary trip, Paul visited the cities of Derbe, Lystra, Iconium and Pisidian Antioch (see *Act. 13–14*). He started churches in these cities. On his second missionary journey, Paul went to the *"region of Galatia"* (*18:6*), which may be to the north. Who did Paul write to? Did he write to churches in the south or the north?

Most likely Paul wrote to churches in the south. Acts gives a clear record that Paul started these churches. Paul likely wrote the book of *Galatians* in AD 48. This makes *Galatians* the earliest of Paul's letters in the New Testament.[10]

Paul wrote because false teachers known as "Judaizers" came to the churches he started. Their teachings did not match Paul's Gospel, and some believers followed them. They taught that people first must follow the law of Moses. Only then could they become believers in Christ. Paul's letter stresses that God saves us by His grace. We do not earn salvation by following the law.

What to watch for:

Key words: revelation, circumcision, tutor, flesh.

Tip: Open your Bible to *Galatians* so you can follow the readings.

1. Paul Announces His Theme and Reason for Writing (*1:1-9*)

    A. <u>Paul Claims Authority</u> (*1:1-2*)
- He has authority because he is an apostle.
- His authority comes from God.

    B. <u>Paul Gives a Greeting</u> (*1:3-9*)
- Paul does not give thanks. In other letters, Paul thanks God for his readers. The situation in Galatia is serious.[11]
- Paul goes directly to his theme—the true Gospel.
  ▶ Christ gave Himself for our sins (*1:3-5*).
  ▶ The Galatians had turned away to follow another Gospel. Paul writes to correct them (*1:6-9*).

2. Paul Defends His Authority (*1:10–2:21*)

    A. <u>Paul's Gospel Comes from God</u> (*1:10-16*)
- Paul did not learn the Gospel from other apostles. He learned directly from Christ (*1:10-16*).

NOTES

"But I make known to you, brethren, that the gospel which was preached by me is not according to man. For I neither received it from man, nor was I taught it, but it came through the revelation of Jesus Christ" (*1:11-12*)

Key Word
Revelation: Paul received his knowledge directly from Christ. He was a witness to the Gospel. His revelation allowed him to see that Christ was God's Son who brought salvation to Jews and Greeks (*1:16; 2:16;* see *Act. 9* for the story of Paul's conversion).

- ▶ Paul used to work against Christians in Judaism, the Jewish way of life based on the Old Testament and other traditions (*1:13-14;* see *Act. 9:1*).
- ▶ Then God called Paul to preach the Gospel (*1:15-16;* see *Act. 9:15*).

As you read Galatians, watch for these verses. Write down the signs of the true Gospel that Paul preached.

- *1:11-12:*

- *2:20:*

- *3:14:*

- *3:21-22:*

- *3:26-28:*

- *5:24-25:*

B. <u>Paul Has the Same Authority as Other Apostles</u> (*1:17–2:21*)
   - After his revelation, Paul did not go to Jerusalem. He did not have to learn from the other apostles because he learned from Christ (*1:17*).
   - After three years, Paul went to Jerusalem to meet with leaders of the church. Then he continued his ministry (*1:18-24;* see *Act. 9:26-28*).
     - ▶ Peter — Paul stayed with him for 15 days (*1:18*).
     - ▶ James — the brother of Jesus (*1:19*). This James was not one of the original disciples. "Apostle" did not always mean the twelve disciples (See *Mat. 10:1-4; 1 Cor. 15:5*).
     - ▶ Paul then went on to Syria and Cilicia in his own ministry. He explains this to prove his authority is from Christ, not other leaders (*1:21-24*).
   - The other apostles know Paul is an apostle (*2:1-10*).

- Paul took a second trip to Jerusalem. He and other leaders discussed the Gospel he preached (*2:1-5*; see *Act. 15:2*).
  - Titus was a Gentile who served with Paul. He was not circumcised.
  - False teachers tried to make people follow the Jewish law, including circumcision. Paul taught Christian freedom.
- The other leaders agreed with Paul. Gentiles did not have to follow Jewish law before they could believe in Christ.
  - God called Paul to preach to the Gentiles (*2:7*).
  - God called Peter to preach to the Jews (*2:8*).
  - *"right hand of fellowship"* — sign of acceptance and friendship (*2:9*).

Key Word
Circumcision: Originally, God gave circumcision as a sign of His covenant with Israel (See *Gen. 17:9-14*). However, it became a sign of following the law, rather than a sign of relationship. Paul says true circumcision is of the heart (See *Rom. 2:25-26; Col. 2:11*).[12]

- Paul had authority to correct other leaders (*2:11-21*).
  - Paul challenged Peter. Peter had suddenly refused to eat with Gentiles. This was part of the Jewish law (*2:12*). (See *Act. 15:35*. Peter fell into the trap of putting himself under human rules — *"the fear of man," Pro. 29:25* — that pulls us away from God's grace).
    - The fear of man is a core sin issue for all men. Peter seemed to struggle with this temptation. Even on the night he denied Jesus three times (*Luk. 22:54-60*) he was motivated by the fear of man.
    - In the Gospels, many of the Jewish leaders would not publicly follow Christ because they feared the rejection of the Pharisees (See *Joh. 5:43-44; 12:42-43*). They wanted the honor of each other rather than the honor that comes only from God. This fear of man hindered their faith. *"The fear of the Lord is the beginning of knowledge"* (*Pro. 1:7*).
  - Leaders had already decided that Gentiles did not have to follow Jewish law. Peter acted as if the Gospel was not for the Gentiles (*2:13-15*).
  - Paul states his message clearly. God declares us "not guilty" by His grace. We are not righteous because of what we do (*2:16-21*).

  "For I through the law died to the law that I might live to God. I have been crucified with Christ; it is no longer I who live, but Christ lives in me, and the life which I now live in the flesh I live by faith in the Son of God, who loved me and gave himself for me" (*2:19-20*).

  - The law shows us we are sinners, but the law is not sinful (*2:18*).
  - The power of Christ lives in us (*2:19-21*; see *Rom. 8:2*).

NOTES

3. Paul Defends Justification by Faith (*3:1–4:31*)

A. <u>Paul Shows the Roots of the Gospel</u> (*3:1-25;* see *Rom. 4:1-25*).
- The Galatians have already heard the truth (*3:1-5*).

"Are you so foolish? Having begun in the Spirit, are you now being made perfect by the flesh?" (3:3).

- ▶ Life in the Spirit does not match up with life in the flesh.
  - ▷ "Spirit" becomes a major theme in Galatians. Paul talks about the Holy Spirit 16 times.
  - ▷ The Spirit works by faith, not by actions that follow the Jewish law (*3:5;* see *Rom. 4:4-5*).
- ▶ *"Suffered so many things in vain"* — This suggests believers in Galatia suffered for their faith in the Gospel before false teachers came.

Key Word:

Flesh: human nature in a condition of weakness without the Holy Spirit. Circumcision was part of life in the "flesh." Without the Spirit, it is only a human attempt to be righteous (See *Rom. 8:1-11*).

- Even Abraham was saved by faith. All who believe, including Gentiles, are children of Abraham (*3:6-9;* see *Gen. 15:6; Rom. 4:1-16*).
- *Hab. 2:4* shows that God declares us "not guilty" by faith. *Lev. 18:5* shows we cannot be saved by keeping the law (*3:10-12;* see also *Deu. 27:26*).
- Christ took the punishment for our guilt (*3:13-14*).
  - ▶ Because of Christ, Gentiles received the blessing of Abraham (*3:14;* see *3:8, Rom. 4:1-16*).
  - ▶ Because of Christ, all who believe receive the promise of the Spirit (*3:14*).
- Jesus Christ fulfills God's promise to Abraham (*3:15-18*).
  - ▶ The covenant was God's relationship with His people (*Gen. 12:2–3:7; 15:18-29; 17:4-8*).
  - ▶ The law came 430 years later. The law does not set aside the covenant. Righteousness comes by faith.
- The purpose of the law is to lead us to Christ (*3:19-25*).

Key Word

Tutor: A tutor had the responsibility to care for a boy and help him learn until he grew up. The law cared for humans until Christ came. The law guides us to Christ (See Rom. 7:14-20).[13]

"But before faith came, we were kept under guard by the law, kept for the faith which would afterward be revealed. Therefore the law was our tutor to bring us to Christ" (3:23-24).

Use your own words to explain the relationship between law and faith.

B. Paul Explains the Advantages and Responsibilities of Sonship (*3:26–4:41*)
- Believers are children of God, without distinctions between them (*3:26-29*).
- Adopted children are true children (*4:1-7;* see *Rom. 8:12-17*).
  - ▶ A child could not make decisions. One day he would inherit, but as a child, he had no more freedom than a slave (*4:1-2*).
  - ▶ *"Bondage under the elements of the world"* — Apart from Christ, we are slaves to principles of the world (*4:3*).
  - ▶ *"Fullness of the time"* — God planned the perfect time in history to send Christ (*4:4*).
    - ▷ Now believers are adopted children with full rights to inherit (*4:5-7;* see *Rom. 5:5; 8:9; 8:15-16*).
- Paul makes a personal request (*4:8-20*).
  - ▶ He tells the Galatians not to turn back to following Jewish laws to become righteous (*4:8-11*).
  - ▶ He asks them to remember their close and loving relationship with him. He brought them the Gospel and they received it (*4:12-20*).
- Paul gives an illustration from history. God promised Abraham a son. Abraham had one son by a slave, Hagar. He had a second son by his wife, Sarah (*4:21-31*).
  - ▶ Hagar's son was born because Abraham tried to make the promise come true. Sarah's son was born because God made the promise come true (*4:22-23*).
  - ▶ The two sons represent two covenants (*4:24-27*).
    - ▷ One is a covenant of law. It leads to slavery. Jerusalem represents this covenant.
    - ▷ The other is a covenant of grace. It leads to freedom. The heavenly Jerusalem represents this covenant (See *Isa. 54:1*).
  - ▶ Paul applies the illustration (*4:28-31*).
    - ▷ The birth of Isaac is like the new birth of Christians (*4:28;* see *Joh. 3:3, 5*).
    - ▷ Ishmael's persecution of Isaac (see *Gen. 21:8-9*) is like the false teachers leading believers the wrong way (*4:29*).
    - ▷ Abraham sent Hagar and Ishmael away. As a result, the Galatians should send the false teachers away (*4:30*).[14]

NOTES

Read *Galatians 4*. Use your own words to explain why Paul does not want believers to go back to the Jewish law.

Are there people in your church plant that are living by law or legalistic rules? How will you minister to them and show them His grace?

NOTES

4. Paul Defends Liberty from the Law (*5:1–6:10*)

A. <u>Do not Misuse the Liberty Christ Gives Us</u> (*5:1-15*)
  - One extreme is "legalism" — following the law to be righteous (*5:1-12*).
    ▶ But no one can keep the whole law (*5:1-4;* see *Rom. 2:25; Rom. 9:31*).

    "For we through the spirit eagerly wait for the hope of righteousness by faith. For in Christ Jesus neither circumcision nor uncircumcision avails anything, but faith working through love" (*5:5-6*).

    ▶ Instead of following the law, we wait for *"the hope of righteousness by faith"* (*5:5-6;* see *Rom. 8:24*).

    "You ran well. Who hindered you from obeying the truth? This persuasion does not come from Him who calls you" (*5:7-8*).

    ▶ *"Leaven"* — was represented by the Judaizers who came to Galatia and influenced believers. They only caused trouble. It only takes a little leaven to affect the whole loaf of bread (*5:7-12*).
  - The other extreme uses freedom as an excuse (*5:13-15*).
    ▶ Christian freedom is not a reason to do whatever we want (*5:13;* see *1 Cor. 8:9*).
    ▶ True Christian freedom is the freedom to serve each other in love (*5:14-15;* see *1 Pet. 2:16*).

B. <u>Walk in the Power of the Holy Spirit</u> (*5:16-26*)
  - The law of the Spirit is opposite to the law of the flesh. The Spirit works in us to overcome the sinful flesh (*5:16-18;* see *Rom. 8:1-11*).
  - Paul lists actions that prove a person is not living by the Spirit (*5:19-21*).
  - Paul lists qualities that prove a person is living by the Spirit. The Spirit bears fruit in the person's life. There is no law against these things (*5:22-23*).
  - *"Crucified with Christ"* — We no longer have to live by the world's values. The Spirit leads us to live by the Spirit's values (*5:24-26;* see *Rom. 6:6*).

How are flesh and Spirit opposite in how we are saved (justification)?

How are flesh and Spirit opposite in how we live after we are saved (sanctification)?

C. Keeping in Step with the Spirit Means Living a Life of Service (*6:1-10*) NOTES
- Serve the person who has sinned (*6:1-4*).
  ▶ *"You who are spiritual"* — The more mature may help the less mature (*6:1-2; see 1 Cor. 3:1-3;* only a spiritual person wants to restore a fallen brother. The person under the influence of human nature wants to judge the fallen person in order to feel superior).
  ▶ *"Law of Christ"* — A summary of the law in *"Love your neighbor"* (*6:2; see 5:14; Mat. 22:39; Joh. 13:35-34*).
  ▶ Be careful. Anyone may fall into sin (*6:3-5*).
- Serve in the work of the Spirit (*6:6-10*).
  ▶ *"Sow" and "reap"* — Living in the flesh will bring judgment. Living in the Spirit will bring life. We do not earn salvation by works, but good works come from the Spirit in our lives (*6:6-8; see 5:19-21*).
  ▶ *"Therefore"* — This word is a clue that Paul expects action. The truth of living in the Spirit will show in our actions toward others.

5. Conclusion (*6:11-18*)

A. Paul Gives a Summary of the Church's Problem — Legalism (6:11-13)
- *"Large letters"* — Paul was so concerned with those who would pervert the Gospel that he wrote this letter with his own hand and with large letters. Paul wanted to make sure the Galatians knew it was he who wrote the letter. Paul was serious about the subject of the true Gospel of pure grace (*6:11*).
- *"Good showing"* — The Judaizers wanted to appear spiritual (*6:12*).
  ▶ So often those who add their own rules and regulations to God's Word seek to establish their own kingdom and *not* God's kingdom.

Adding or subtracting anything from God's Word or the Gospel message will always result in heresy. When you preach do you ever add or subtract from your message to make it easier for people to accept? Discuss.

- *"Boast in your flesh"* — The Judaizers wanted to boast that they had followers (*6:13*).
  ▶ The cross of Christ crushes any right to boast that we can save ourselves by our works. The cross of Christ has paid it all.

B. Paul Gives a Summary of the Solution — Christ (6:14-15)
- *"Cross of our Lord Jesus Christ"* — final summary of the Gospel (*6:14*).
- *"New creation"* — circumcision or other Jewish laws mean nothing. Only the work of Christ matters (*6:15*).

C. Paul Closes with a Blessing (*6:16-18*)

Suggestions for Preaching from *Galatians*

- Explore the major themes of *Galatians*: law, faith, freedom, the Holy Spirit.

- Use *Galatians* as a starting point to teach on misunderstandings of Christian doctrine and how to guard against them.

- Compare positive actions and attitudes in *Galatians* with negative actions and attitudes.

Chapter Five
Ephesians

Ephesus was the capital city of the Roman province of Asia. Now this area is part of Turkey. Several main trade routes met in Ephesus. Paul visited Ephesus at the end of his second missionary journey. He left Aquila and Priscilla to lead the church there (*Act. 18:18-21*). Later, on Paul's third journey, he spent about three years in Ephesus. He used the city as a center for his work in the region. So many people in Ephesus believed in Jesus that the businessmen started a riot (*Act. 19:21-41*). These men earned money by making and selling idols.

The letter to the *Ephesians* has general themes. It does not have the personal nature of many of Paul's letters. Most likely Paul wanted people in several different churches to read the letter. He has not met many of these people, so he cannot write to them in a personal way.

The first half of the letter talks about key beliefs of the Christian faith. The second half describes how beliefs turn into actions. Paul urged readers to live in a way that showed they were joined to Christ. Paul wrote the letter while he was a prisoner in Rome; around AD 60.[15] The themes of *Colossians* and *Ephesians* are similar. Paul wrote both letters about the same time.

What to watch for:

Key Words: purpose, new man, submission.

Tip: Open your Bible to *Ephesians* so you can follow the readings.

1. Spiritual Blessings of the Church (*1:1–3:21*)

God does not promise human riches to the believer, but He does promise spiritual blessings.

A. <u>Paul Gives a Greeting of Grace</u> (*1:1-2*)
   - Paul gives a common greeting and also makes his authority plain. He is an apostle of Jesus Christ by the will of God. Here he declares his position and his calling to his position.
   - Also, Paul speaks on behalf of God, the Father of our Lord Jesus Christ.

B. <u>God Shows a Plan for His people Through the Trinity</u> (*1:3-14*)
   - God the Father chose believers (*1:4-5*).
     ▶ "Chose," "predestined" — a common theme in Paul's letters (See *Rom. 8:29-33; 9:6-26; 11:5; 7, 28; 16:13; Col. 3:12; 1 The. 1:4; 2 The. 2:13; Tit. 1:1*).

NOTES

Key Word

Purpose: Paul uses three related words in *1:11* — *"purpose"* (see *Rom. 8:38; Eph. 1:9*), *"counsel"* (see *1 Cor. 4:5; Heb. 6:17*), and *"will"* (see *Eph. 2:3; 5:17; Rom. 1:10*). The main idea is that behind God's will is His heart of love.[16] God's *decretive* will is what God planned, or intended from the foundation of the world. Much of God's decretive will is kept secret until He reveals it at the right time (See *Deu. 29:29; Rom. 11:33*). God's *prescriptive* will is what He commands, or prescribes, for us to do, such as the Ten Commandments.

- The Son rescued believers (*1:5-12*).
  ▶ Believers have redemption, forgiveness, grace, wisdom, prudence.
  ▶ *"Dispensation of the fullness of the times"* — This word means "house rule." God arranged history to fulfill His plan of salvation. The plan has different phases. Here Paul means the time when God will set up His eternal kingdom.[17]
- The Holy Spirit makes sure God's promise of eternal life. He guarantees our inheritance (*1:13-14;* see *Rom. 8:23; Col. 1:12; Heb. 9:15*).

C. Paul Prays for Spiritual Wisdom (*1:15-22*)
   - *"Heard of your faith"* — Paul has not met all these readers (*1:15*).
   - *"The eyes of your understanding"* — inner, spiritual understanding (*1:18*).

"...that you may know what is the hope of His calling, what are the riches of the glory of His inheritance in the saints, and what is the exceeding greatness of His power toward us who believe" (*1:18-19*).

Name the elements of Paul's prayer for the Ephesians. How can you use these elements as you pray for family and friends? Who can pray this type of prayer for you?

Why do you think Paul gives emphasis to God's purpose and plan?

- The same power that raised Christ from the dead works in us (*1:19b-21*).
- In the end, Christ will rule over everything. This is God's final purpose (*1:22-23;* see *Col. 2:9; Heb. 2:7*).

D. <u>Salvation Is by Grace through Faith</u> (*2:1-10*)
- In our old nature, we were dead to God. We followed the ways of our sinful nature (*2:1-3*).
- In our new nature, we are alive to God (*2:4-10*).
  - ▶ God has great love and mercy. He made us alive in Christ (*2:4;* see *Rom. 6:1-10*).
  - ▶ *"In the heavenly places in Christ Jesus"* — Our union with Christ lasts for eternity (*2:6;* see *Eph. 1:20*).

"For by grace you have been saved through faith, and that not of yourselves; it is the gift of God, not of works, lest anyone should boast. For we are His workmanship, created in Christ Jesus for good works, which God prepared beforehand that we should walk in them" (*2:8-10*).

  - ▶ Salvation comes from the grace of God, not by human effort.
    - ▷ *"have been saved"* — past tense. Salvation is a finished action (See *Rom. 3:21-31*).
    - ▷ *"workmanship"* — This word means "a thing made,"[18] such as a work of art. The church is God's creative work (See *Psa. 19:1; Rom. 1:20*).
  - ▶ *"Prepared in advance"* — the theme of God's purpose and plan, as in Chapter 1.

E. <u>Jews and Gentiles Are One Body in Christ</u> (*2:11-22*)
- *"Uncircumcision"* and *"Circumcision"* — Gentiles and Jews.
  - ▶ Gentiles once had no hope because they were not part of God's people. Through Christ, God has brought them to Himself (*2:11-12*).
  - ▶ *"Middle wall of separation"* — In the Jewish temple, Gentiles could worship only in the outer court. They did not worship with Jews. This wall represented the separation between them (*2:14*).
    - ▷ *"in His flesh"* — the death of Christ did away with the separation. Christ kept the law no human could keep (*2:15*).
    - ▷ *"one new man from the two"* — The Christian church now included both Gentiles and Jews (*2:16-18*).

"Now, therefore, you are no longer strangers and foreigners, but fellow citizens with the saints and members of the household of God" (*2:19*)

  - ▶ *"Foundation"* — The apostles are the foundation of the church, but Christ Himself is the rock that holds the building together (*2:19-22*).

NOTES

NOTES   **Why is the unity of believers important to Paul?**

Why should the unity of believers be important to us?

F. <u>The Mystery of Christ's Body</u> (*3:1-21*)
- God unites all believers in one body (*3:1-13*).
  ▶ *"Mystery"* — truth that comes from God (*3:3*).
  ▶ *"In other ages"* — People in earlier times of history had knowledge of God (*3:5*).
    ▷ This knowledge was *not* the "revelation."
    ▷ The Holy Spirit revealed the mystery to early church leaders.
  ▶ The mystery is that Gentiles share in salvation with the Jews (*3:6*).
  ▶ *"Less than the least"* — Paul was always humble about the special work God called him to do. His ministry was to preach to the Gentiles (*3:8;* see *1 Tim. 1:15*).
  ▶ The church's unity shows God's plan. Now Christ is head of the church. At the end of time, the whole world will see He is head of the universe (*3:11-13;* see *Phi. 2:9-11*).
- Paul prays for all the Ephesians, whether Gentiles or Jews (*3:14-21*).

"...that Christ may dwell in your hearts through faith; that you, being rooted and grounded in love, may be able to comprehend with all the saints what is the width and length and depth and height—to know the love of Christ which passes knowledge" (*3:17-18*).

  ▶ *"Dwell"* — Christ lives in the believer's heart.
  ▶ The love of Christ is beyond our understanding (*3:19*).
  ▶ *"To Him be glory in the church"* — The goal of the church is to bring glory to God (*3:21*).

Read these verses from *Ephesians*. Write down what each verse tells us about our identity in Christ.

NOTES

- *1:3:*

- *1:4:*

- *1:5-6:*

- *1:7:*

- *2:6:*

- *2:10:*

- *2:13:*

- *3:6:*

- *3:12:*

2. Responsibilities of the Church (*4:1–6:24*)

Spiritual blessings for believers bring responsibilities toward one another.

A. <u>Believers Should Pursue Unity of the Spirit</u> (*4:1-6*)
   - *"Therefore"* — Believing the truth leads to changes in action. We only truly believe what we seek to live (*4:1-3; see 1 The. 2:12*).
   - One Holy Spirit unites believers. Gentiles and Jews come together in Christ. Paul repeats the word "one" to stress unity (*4:4-6; see Rom. 12:5*).

B. <u>Believers Use Gifts to Build Up the Church</u> (*4:7-16*)

"But to each one of us grace was given according to the measure of Christ's gift" (*4:7*).

- *"Each one"* — Every believer has a gift or gifts. The gift comes by God's grace. Every believer uses a gift according to how Christ allows (*4:7*).
- *"Ascended on high"* — from *Psa. 68:18*. The Messiah triumphs over Satan (*4:8*). Jesus is the Victorious Warrior.
  ▶ *"Lower parts of the earth"* — Christ came to earth as a human (*4:9; see Phi. 2:5-8*).
  ▶ One day the world will see that Christ is supreme (*4:10; see Phi. 2:9-11; Col. 1:18*).
- Christ, who is supreme, gives the gifts (*4:11-16*).
  ▶ Paul names five kinds of gifts/gifted people:
    ▷ *Apostles* — those chosen by Christ to establish the church.[19]
    ▷ *Prophets* — gave messages from God.

NOTES

▷ *Evangelists* — those who preach the Gospel.
▷ *Pastors* — care for the church, as a shepherd cares for sheep.
▷ *Teachers* — systematic, line by line communicators.

"...till we all come to the unity of the faith and of the knowledge of the Son of God, to a perfect man, to the measure of the stature of the fullness of Christ...but speaking the truth in love, may grow up in all things into Him who is the head—Christ" (4:13-16).

- Jesus and Paul desire the church to be built on persons and not one personality. There is unity and sharing in the Trinity. There must be unity and sharing in the local church, gifted leaders who share in equipping/coaching the saints to do the work of the ministry. One person may be the leader, but he is to share the load and equip fully with other gifted leaders.
  ▶ When believers use the gifts Christ gives, the church grows.
    ▷ *"for works of ministry"* — *(4:12).*
    ▷ *"edifying of the body"* — *(4:12).*
    ▷ Spiritual maturity for the church body *(4:13-16).*

C. <u>Believers Put on the New Person and Walk in Holiness</u> *(4:17-32)*
  - *"No longer walk,"* — We take off the ways of the "old man." *(4:17-19; see 2:1-3).*
  - *"You have not so learned"* — Paul stresses the change from the old man to the new man *(4:20-23).*

  "...that you put off, concerning your former conduct, the old man which grows corrupt according to the deceitful lusts, and be renewed in the spirit of your mind, and put on the new man which was created according to God, in true righteousness and holiness" (4:22-24).

  - *"Put on the new man"* — In Christ, believers are new people. We *"put on"* an experience of Christ's righteousness, and this shows in our lives *(4:24; see Rom. 6:2-10; 2 Cor. 5:17).*
  - Paul lists examples of changes in attitude and action in the new man *(4:25-32; see Rom. 12:5).*

Key Word
New Man: "New" does not mean newer in time. It means "different in nature." The new man is the new humanity created in Christ (See *Col. 3:9-11*).

D. <u>Believers Imitate God</u> *(5:1-21)*
  - Walk in love *(5:1-7).*
    ▶ God loved us and sent Christ to save us. Christ loved us and gave Himself for us. Love should be our guiding principle in every situation *(5:1).*
      ▷ In the Old Testament, a *"sweet-smelling aroma"* in sacrifice pleased God (See *Gen. 8:21; Exo. 29:18, 25, 41; Lev. 1:9, 13, 17*).
    ▶ Do not fall into the values of the pagan world *(5:3-7; see Rom. 1:19-31; Col. 3:5-7).*

- Walk as children of light (*5:8-14*).

"For you were once darkness, but now you are light in the Lord. Walk as children of light" (*5:8*).

  ▶ *"You were once," "now you are"* — Again, Paul points out the change that comes with being in Christ (*5:8*).
  ▶ Christ's light shines in our actions. We belong to the light and it shows in our lives. Do not get mixed up with the works of those who do evil (*5:9-14; see Gal. 22-23*).
- Be wise in God's purpose (*5:15-17*).
  ▶ *"Not as fools but as wise"* — This is another way to show the difference between the old man and the new man, between light and darkness (*5:15-16*).
  ▶ The unwise do not understand God's purpose (*5:17;* see Paul's explanation of God's purpose in *Eph. 1:1–3:21*).
- Live in the Spirit (*5:18-21*).

"Do not be drunk with wine, in which is dissipation; but be filled with the Spirit" (*5:18*).

  ▶ *"Be filled"* — The Spirit influences our actions and relationships.

E. <u>Believers Live in Relationship to Each Other</u> (*5:22–6:9*)
- Relationships between husbands and wives (*5:22-33*).
  ▶ A woman who submits to her husband also submits to the Lord (*5:22-24*).
    ▷ Christ's relationship with the church is an example for marriage relationships (See *Col. 1:18*).
  ▶ Husbands follow Christ's example of self-sacrifice and love (*5:25-29*).
    ▷ Love looks to the best for someone else.
    ▷ Christ's sacrifice was for the good of the church. He wanted to make the church what God wanted it to be.

    "…that He might present her to Himself a glorious church, not having spot or wrinkle or any such thing, but that she should be holy and without blemish" (*5:27*).

    ▷ This love is the example for husbands to follow.

Key Word
Submission: This word has military origins. One person chooses to be under the authority of another person. Paul stresses the duty of the person in authority. The relationship between Christ and the church is the model (See *1 Pet. 2:1; 5:5; Col. 3:18-23*).[20]

- Relationships between children and parents (*6:1-4*).
  ▶ When children obey parents, they honor the Lord (*6:1;* see *Pro. 30:17; Col. 3:20*).
  ▶ Paul's command reflects one of the Ten Commandments (*6:2-3;* see *Deu. 5:16*).

NOTES

- ▶ Parents should be reasonable with their children (*6:4*).
  - ▷ Rules without a relationship will cause rebellion (See *Pro. 23:26*).
  - ▷ Affection comes first, and then example. This is the best way to lead a child.
- Relationships between slaves and masters (*6:5-9*).
  - ▶ Many people in the Roman Empire were slaves. Paul does not speak for or against slavery. He simply speaks to people who are slaves (*6:5*).
  - ▶ *"As to Christ"* — Once again, Paul says submission to another person honors the Lord (*6:5-6*).
  - ▶ *"Receive the same"* — God is the final judge (*5:7-8;* see *1 Pet. 1:17*).
  - ▶ Masters, also, must honor the Lord in relationships with slaves (*5:9*).

F. <u>Believers Put on the Whole Armor of God</u> (*6:10-20*)

"Finally, my brethren, be strong in the Lord and in the power of His might. Put on the whole armor of God, that you may be able to stand against the wiles of the devil" (*6:10-11*).

- As a prisoner in Rome, Paul probably knew the armor well.[21]
- God's armor protects the believer against evil and the Evil One (*6:10-13*).
- The unseen spiritual world is real.
  - ▶ *"Flesh and blood"* — The Christian's real battle is not against human false teachers. The real battle is against the devil and demons (*6:12*).
    - ▷ *"principalities," "powers," "rulers of the darkness of this age," "spiritual hosts of wickedness."*
    - ▷ Paul earlier discussed powerful beings in world's humans cannot see (See *1:21; 3:10*).
- Paul describes the pieces of armor.
  - ▶ *"Having girded your waist with truth"* — Strips of leather hung from the belt. This protected the lower body. For the Christian, truth wins the battle, rather than force (*6:14*).
  - ▶ *"Breastplate of righteousness"* — hard leather or metal. This went all the way around the body. For the Christian, character provides defense (*6:14*).
  - ▶ *"Having shod your feet with the preparation of the gospel"* — hard shoes. The Christian is ready to spread the Gospel (*6:15*).
  - ▶ *"Shield of faith"* — offers protection against weapons of the enemy. Satan's attacks cannot hurt the person with faith in God (*6:16*).
  - ▶ *"Helmet of salvation"* — protected the head. The helmet can also be a symbol of victory in battle (*6:17*).
  - ▶ *"Sword of the Spirit"* — a reminder that the battle is spiritual (*6:17*).[22]

This spiritual battle is offensive in nature, we can be on the offensive at all times in the Spirit.

Why does Paul stress putting on the "whole" armor of God? What happens if a soldier only wears part of the armor?

NOTES

- Without prayer, the armor is useless (*6:18*).
  - Paul asks the Ephesians to pray for him.
  - He wants to make known the *"mystery of the gospel."* Mystery is a key theme for Paul (See *Eph. 3:3, 9; Col. 4:3*). In the past God's plan for salvation was hidden. Now God reveals it.
  - Even as a prisoner, Paul preaches the Gospel (*6:20*).

3. Paul's Blessing (*6:21-24*)

Suggestions for Preaching from *Ephesians*

- Teach on the reality of spiritual warfare.

- Explore verses about our true identity in Christ.

- Study the characteristics of relationships that honor God.

- Explore how to promote diversity and unity in the church body.

- Pray for your new church and the Lord's activity through His Holy Spirit to protect each of you in your congregation from the deceit of the devil.

Chapter Six
Philippians

NOTES

Paul started the church in Philippi on his second missionary journey (See *Act. 16:6-12*). Philippi was the leading city in Macedonia. It held the status of a Roman colony. Philippi was located on the Egnatian Way. This was the main road across Greece on the way to Rome.

The church was a mixture of people from different races and cultures. The first person to believe was a wealthy woman named Lydia (*Act. 16:14-15*). She was followed by a Roman jailer (*Act. 16:22-34*). Also, a lower-class girl controlled by a demon perhaps believed (*Act. 16:16-18*). Church members primarily were Gentiles.

Paul wrote the letter to the *Philippians* from the city of Rome. He was in prison at the time, but he wrote about great joy and partnership in ministry. The Philippians had many areas of strength. Paul wrote to them to encourage them for their progress and to keep growing in weak areas. Paul uses Jesus' life as the model for believers. This short letter encourages believers today as well.[23]

What to watch for:

Key Words: joy/rejoice, humility, peace.

Tip: Open your Bible to *Philippians* so you can follow the readings.

1. Paul Prays for the Philippians (*1:3-11*)

  A. <u>Paul Thanks God for the Philippians</u> (1:1-5)
   * Paul made a special mention of the *"bishops and deacons"*, who were included with *"all the saints."* The bishops were the overseers or elders (See *Tit. 1:5, 7*); and were responsible for shepherding the church. The deacons were the church leaders who served among the church (*1:1;* see *Act. 6; 20:17, 28*)
   * Paul often begins his letters with prayers of thanksgiving (See *Rom. 1:8; 1 Cor. 1:4; Col. 1:3; 1 The. 1:2; 2 The. 1:3; 2 Tim. 1:3; Phm. 4*).
   * *"Fellowship"* — This term usually means a business partnership. Paul recognizes the Philippians' support of his ministry (*1:5*).[24]

  B. <u>Paul is Confident of the Work Christ Does</u> (*1:6-8*)
   * God's work continues in the hearts of believers until Christ returns (*1:6*).
   * *"In my chains"* — Paul writes from prison (*1:7*).

  C. <u>Paul Prays for the Philippians to Grow Spiritually</u> (*1:9-11*)
   * *"That your love may abound"* — the highest form of Christian love (1:9).[25]
   * *"Fruits of righteousness"* — changes that come from God declaring us *"not guilty."*

NOTES **How do these opening verses show us that prayer can encourage us?**

2. Paul Explains His Ministry (*1:12-26*)

A. <u>Even in Prison, Paul Preaches</u> (*1:12-18*)

"But I want you to know, brethren, that the things which happened to me have actually turned out for the furtherance of the gospel" (*1:12*).

- Being in prison helps the Gospel to spread, rather than hurting it (*1:12-14*).
  - ▶ *"Palace guard"* — The Gospel is spreading in the Roman military (*1:12-14*).
  - ▶ *"All the rest"*—The Gospel is spreading beyond Paul's prison to other parts of Rome.
  - ▶ *"Encouraged to speak"*—Other believers are sharing the Gospel boldly too (*1:14*).
- Preaching must be from the right motive (*1:15-18*).
  - ▶ *"From envy and strife,"* *"selfish ambition,"* *"add affliction"* — Some preachers looked for attention and caused trouble for Paul (*1:15-16*).
  - ▶ *"Goodwill,"* *"out of love"* — Others had better motives (*1:15, 17*).
  - ▶ *"Only that in every way"* — Paul was pleased to see the Gospel spreading, even when the motive to preach was not pure (*1:18*).

B. <u>Bring Glory to Christ</u> (*1:19-26;* see *Eph. 6:19-20*).
- Paul has a positive attitude because he knows God will work (*1:19*).
  - ▶ *"Turn out for my deliverance"* — This word is also translated "salvation" "healing" or "rescue from danger."[26]
  - ▶ *"To live is Christ, and to die is gain"* — Even if Paul dies while in prison, Paul's life would bring glory to God (*1:21-24;* see *2 Cor. 5:1, 8*).

"For I am hard-pressed between the two, having a desire to depart and be with Christ, which is far better. Nevertheless to remain in the flesh is more needful for you" (*2:23-24*).

- ▶ *"Flesh"* — In this verse, the word means simply physical body. Paul puts the needs of the Philippians above his own desire to be with Christ (*2:24*).
- ▶ *"Progress and joy in the faith"* — After coming to Christ, Christians grow to be more mature in Christ (*2:26;* see *1:9*).

3. A Call to Worthy Conduct (1:27–2:18)

NOTES

A. <u>Strive for Christian Unity in the Gospel</u> (*1:27-30*)
   - *"Conduct"* — Philippi was a Roman colony. The citizens understood the responsibilities of citizenship. Live in this world as citizens of the heavenly kingdom.[27] (See *Eph. 4:1*).
   - *"Proof of perdition"* — With their lives, Christians prove the Gospel is true (*1:28*).

B. <u>Share a Humble Attitude</u> (*2:1-11*)
   - Believers should seek unity through humility.

"Let nothing be done through selfish ambition or conceit, but in lowliness of mind let each esteem others better than himself" (2:3).

   ▶ Honest self-examination leads to humility (*2:4–5;* see *1 Cor. 13:5; Rom. 15:1-2*).
   - Share the attitude of Christ (*2:5-11*).

"Let this mind be in you which was also in Christ Jesus, who, being in the form of God, did not consider it robbery to be equal with God, but made Himself of no reputation, taking form of a bondservant, and coming in the likeness of men. And being found in appearance as a man, He humbled Himself and became obedient to the point of death, even death of the cross" (2:5-8).

   ▶ *"Form of God"* — the way something exists, what it truly is. Christ was fully God (*2:6*).
   ▶ *"Made himself of no reputation"* — Christ did not give up being God. Instead, he gave up the glory of being God (*2:7;* see *Joh. 17:5; 2 Cor. 8:9*).
   ▶ *"Likeness of men"* — Jesus did not simply look like a human. He was human (See *Joh. 1:14; Rom. 8:3; Heb. 2:17*).

Key Word
Humility: As God, Jesus held a position of power. He moved to a position of weakness. He did not boast or make claims. Instead, He made Himself lower and became a servant. *Phi. 2:5-11* is the most famous passage in the New Testament about humility.

"Therefore God also has highly exalted Him and given Him the name which is above every name, that at the name of Jesus every knee should bow, of those in heaven, and of those on earth, and of those under the earth, and that every tongue should confess that Jesus Christ is Lord, to the glory of God the Father" (2:9-11).

   ▶ Jesus humbled Himself. God raised him up. Christ is Lord (*2:9;* see *Mat. 28:18; Act. 2:33; Isa. 52:13*).
   ▶ One day everyone will worship Christ (*2:10*).
   ▶ *"Confess"* — a strong verb that means "agree with." Everyone will agree with what God has already said is true (*2:11*).[28]

NOTES   **Use your own words to explain *Philippians 2:5-11*.**

- Respond to Christ's example (*2:12-18*).
  ▶ *"Work out your salvation"* — This phrase comes from the idea of digging silver out of mines.[29] The gift of salvation is ongoing. The believer is involved (*2:12;* see *Mat. 24:13; 1 Cor. 9:24-27; Heb. 3:14; 6:9-11; 2 Pet 1:5-8*).
  ▶ *"God who works in you"* — We depend on God's power (*2:13*).
  ▶ *"Poured out"* — Paul is poured out as a living offering for the Philippians (*2:17;* see *Exo. 29:38-41* for the Old Testament background).
  ▶ Paul refused to do some things.
    ▷ Paul refused to live in *pretense and pride* (*2:3-8; 3:3-13; Gal. 6:14*). Paul did not brag on his ritual, race, religious zeal, or rank.
    ▷ Paul refused to live in the *past tense* (*3:13-14*). Past failure can paralyze us with fear of future failure and lack of esteem. Past success can puff us up and make us complacent.
    ▷ Paul refused to live in the *passive tense* (*3:11-14*). Notice the aggressive words: *"I press forward," "I take hold of," "I strain."* Paul uses words in other books such as *wrestle, run, box,* and *fight*.
    ▷ Paul refused to live a *powerless life* (*3:10; 4:13*). By any means Paul wants this power.
    ▷ Paul refused to live a life without *peace* (*4:1-3; 6-7, 9-11*). He wants peace within the local church among the people (*2:1-4; 4:1-3*). He wants peace within his own heart (*4:6-7*).
    ▷ Paul refused to live a life without *prayer* (*4:6*).
    ▷ Paul refused to live a life without *praise* (*4:4, 8, 20; Neh. 9:10*). Consider how often Paul uses the words *joy, rejoice* and *thanks*. He gives praise for God and God's people.

C. <u>Timothy and Epaphroditus Are Examples of Faithful Service</u> (2:19-30)
- Timothy was with Paul on his second missionary journey. They started the church in Philippi together (See *Act. 16:1; 18:5; 19:22*).
- Paul plans to send Timothy to Philippi. The Philippians knew Timothy well (*2:23-23*).
- Epaphroditus came from Philippi. The Philippians sent him to Paul with a gift (See *4:18*).
- While he was in Rome, Epaphroditus was very ill. Paul stresses the work of Epaphroditus for the Gospel (*2:27-29*).

4. Paul Rejects the World (*3:1-21*)

A. <u>Paul Puts His Confidence in Christ</u> (*3:1-11*)

NOTES

- Rejoice in the Lord, not in human efforts (*1:1-6*).
  - ▶ *"Dogs"* — a harsh word to describe those who work against the Gospel (*3:2-3*).
  - ▶ *"Circumcision"* — true circumcision is by faith (*3:3;* see *Rom. 2:28-29*).

  "If anyone else thinks he has reason to put confidence in the flesh, I have more" (3:4b).

  - ▶ If human effort could save, Paul would be the best according to Jewish law (*3:4-6*).
- Consider everything according to Christ, not human standards (*1:7-11*).

"But what things were gain to me, these I have counted loss for Christ. Yet indeed I also count all things loss for the excellence of the knowledge of Christ Jesus my Lord, for whom I have suffered the loss of all things, and count them as rubbish, that I may gain Christ" (3:7-9).

  - ▶ *"Loss," "rubbish"* — things that have no more use. Knowing Jesus is more valuable than anything else (*3:7-9;* see *Isa. 64:6*).
  - ▶ *"My own righteousness"* — Paul rejects human attempts to be right with God. True righteousness comes by faith (*3:9*).
  - ▶ *"Attain to"* — Here this phrase means "arrive at." Paul expects to experience resurrection because he is united with Christ (*3:11;* see *1 Cor. 15:1-34*).

List some things people do not want to "count as loss."

From Paul's example what happens when we want Jesus more than anything else?

B. <u>Paul Looks Forward, Not Backward</u> (*3:12-21*)

"...one thing I do, forgetting those things which are behind and reaching forward to those things which are ahead, I press toward the goal for the prize of the upward call of God in Christ Jesus" (3:14).

- Paul presses on toward the goal (*3:12-16*).
  - ▶ *"Attained"* — Verse 12 uses a different Greek word than in *3:11*. Here it means "gain possession of."[30]

77

NOTES

- ▸ *"Prize"* — In a race, the winner receives a prize. The Christian receives eternal life (*3:14*). (See *1 Cor. 9:24*).
- ▸ *"To the degree we have already attained"* — practice the truth we already have as we continue to grow.
- Our citizenship is in heaven (*3:17–4:1*).
    - ▸ *"Enemies of the cross"* — Paul weeps for those who preach the law and not grace (*3:18-19*).

"Our citizenship is in heaven, from which we also eagerly wait for the Savior, the Lord Jesus Christ, who will transform our lowly body that it may be conformed to His glorious body" (*3:20-21*).

- ▸ We live in this world, but we are citizens of heaven.
- ▸ See *3:10*: *"conformed to his death."* Here believers are conformed to Christ's life. We will have resurrection bodies (*3:21*).

C. <u>United and Joyful in Prayer</u> (*4:1-9*)
- *"Euodia"* and *"Synteche"* — women in Philippi who did not agree with each other. Paul does not agree with one or the other. He simply urges them to work out their problem (*4:2-3*).
- *"Rejoice in the Lord always"* — Even when we suffer, we can rejoice (*4:4*; see *Hab. 3:17-18*).

Key Word

Joy/Rejoice: Joy does not come from circumstances. It comes from Christ. When Paul calls for joy, he calls for faith (in the Lord; see *1 The. 5:16; Rom. 12:12; Psa. 85:6*). Real Joy is not what we pursue, but a result of being in a right relationship with God the Father, through Jesus the Son, in the fullness of the Holy Spirit!

"Let your gentleness be known to all men. The Lord is at hand" (*4:5*).

- The Lord may return at any moment. This is the next great event in God's plan of salvation (*4:5*; see *Rom. 13:11; Jas. 5:8-9; Rev. 22:7, 12, 20*).

Key Word

Peace: This word appears in each book in the New Testament except *1 John*. An inner quietness results from faith in Christ. The right type of praying and the right type of thinking will produce the peace of God ruling over our hearts and minds no matter the difficulties we face.

- *"meditate on these things"* ... *"these do"* — What we think about will show in our actions (*4:8-9*).

How can joy make a difference in suffering?

How can joy make a difference in serving?

5. Blessings and Benediction (*4:10-23*)

   A. Blessings for Paul (*4:10-18*)
      - The Philippians' gift to Paul has blessed him. Paul is content no matter what, but he is glad to have their gift.
      - Paul commends the Philippians' care for him because it represents spiritual fruit in their lives (*4:17*).

   B. Blessings for the Philippians (*4:19-20*)
      - God will care for the Philippians with His riches in glory (See *Eph. 1:18; 3:16-20*).

   C. Traditional Benediction and Greetings (*4:21-23*)

Godly contentment is the opposite of covetousness. A coveting heart can cause a person to break all the Ten Commandments. See if you can list each of the commandments and explain how we might break them because of coveting.

1.

2.

3.

4.

5.

6.

7.

8.

9.

10.

Suggestions for Preaching From *Philippians*

- Look for the ways we find joy in our daily lives.

- Explore how humility and self-sacrifice connect to life with other Christians, and with non-believers.

NOTES

Chapter Seven
Colossians

The church in Colosse most likely came into being through Paul's ministry in Ephesus. Colosse was a hundred miles east of Ephesus. Paul stayed in Ephesus for three years. A man named Epaphras became a Christian and took the Gospel to Colosse (*1:7-8; Act. 19:10*). This made Paul the "grandfather" of the church in Colosse. The Christians in Colosse were non-Jews. Paul wrote to the *Colossians* while he was a prisoner in Rome, around AD 60. Paul also wrote the letters of *Ephesians*, *Philippians* and *Philemon* while he was in Rome.[31]

The Colossians had fallen into false teaching that blended several human philosophies. These included Jewish law, Greek religion and mystery cults. In the next century, this false teaching would be called "Gnosticism." Gnostics said Christ did not have a body. They separated the spiritual realm from the physical realm. In response to these wrong teachings, Paul emphasized that Christ is supreme in everything and in every way, including salvation.

What to watch for:

Key words: wisdom, firstborn, mystery, fullness, image.

False Teaching and True Correction

Tip: Open your Bible to *Colossians* so you can follow the readings.

1. Supremacy of Christ in the Life of the Colossians (*1:1-14*)

A. <u>Paul Thanks God for the Colossian's Faith in Christ</u> (*1:3-8*)
- Introduction
  - ▶ Paul calls himself an apostle of Christ Jesus. Christ is the focus of the letter from the very beginning (*1:1*).
  - ▶ "Saints" — holy people, set apart to God. Believers are not saints because they are perfect. They are saints because they belong to God (1:2).
- Paul expresses care and love for the Colossians (1:3).
- Paul has heard reports of their faith and love (1:4-6).
  - ▶ Paul often uses *"faith," "love"* and *"hope"* together (See *Rom. 5:2-5; 1 Cor. 13:13; 1 The. 1:3; 5:8*).
    - ▷ *Faith* is in Jesus Christ.
    - ▷ *Love* shows that faith is genuine.
    - ▷ *Faith* and *love* result from the sure *hope* of salvation, the Gospel.
- The Colossians are an example of the fruit the Gospel bears (*1:7-8*).
  - ▶ Epaphras took the Gospel to Colosse, who also told Paul of their love.

NOTES

NOTES   **Read *Colossians 1:3-11*. Write your thoughts on the example Paul gives for praying for others.**

    B. Paul Prays for the Colossians' Understanding (*1:9-14*)
- Paul wants the Colossians to have wisdom and understanding (*1:9*).
  - ▶ *"Filled"* — completeness.
  - ▶ Knowledge of God's will comes through spiritual understanding. The Holy Spirit is at work.
  - ▶ This is an excellent prayer to pray for friends and family.

Key Word
Wisdom: Insight or knowledge that God gives to those who are close to Him (*1:9; 1:28; 2:3; 2:23; 3:16; 4:5*).

- The result of this knowledge and wisdom is a life that pleases God. God gives strength out of His own power (*1:10-11*).
- Paul summarizes redemption. God saves us, and believers are changed. We move from darkness to light (*1:12–14*).

2. Christ Is Supreme in His Nature and Work (*1:15-29*)

    A. Christ Is Supreme Over All Things (*1:15-20*)
- God is invisible, but Christ shows us God exactly. If we want to see what God is like, we look to Jesus.
- Christ is supreme over creation.
  - ▶ He is not a created being. He took part in creation (*1:15-16*).
  - ▶ Christ existed before creation (*1:17*).
- Christ is supreme over all things, including the church (*1:18*).

"For it pleased the Father that in Him all the fullness should dwell, and by Him to reconcile all things to Himself, by Him, whether things on earth or things in heaven, having made peace through the blood of His cross" (*1:19-20*).

- *"Fullness"* — Christ has the complete divine nature. He is fully God. He is a complete picture of God (*1:19*).
- *"Reconcile all things to Himself"* (*1:20*).
  - ▶ This does not mean all people are saved. Christ made it possible for us to have peace with God, but not all believe.
  - ▶ In the future, God will redeem the physical world (See *Rom. 8:19-20*).

Key Word
Firstborn: a title of honor that shows Jesus is supreme. He is first over creation and first in resurrection.

False Teaching and True Correction
False teachers said Christ was one spirit among many. Paul says Christ is supreme above all things. False teachers said Jesus did not have a physical body. Paul says redemption came through Christ's physical death.

    B.   Christ's Work is Glorious (*1:21-23*)
- Paul stresses that salvation comes because of Christ's physical death (*1:21-22*).

"And you, who once were alienated and enemies in your mind by wicked works, yet now He has reconciled in the body of His flesh through death, to present you holy, and blameless, and above reproach in His sight" (*1:21-22*).

▶ Reconciliation is complete. Continuing faith is proof (*1:22; see 2 Cor. 5:18*).
▶ This is the heart of the Gospel (*1:23; see Eph. 3:17*).

3. Christ is Supreme in Paul's Ministry (*1:24–2:7*)

    A.   Christ Motivates Paul's Ministry (*1:24–27*)
- *"fill up in my flesh what is still lacking"* — (*1:24*).
  ▶ Since Christ suffered, believers can expect to suffer (See *2 Cor. 1:5; 4:11*).
  ▶ Paul suffered again and again for Christ (See *2 Cor. 11:23-27*).
- *"The mystery which has been hidden"* — Paul's ministry proclaims the mystery of Christ's death and God's plan for salvation (*1:25–27; see 2 Cor. 2:14*).

Key Word
Mystery: False teachers used this word to mean secret information. Paul uses the word to mean the truth that God revealed in Christ.

    B.   Paul's Goal is Right Teaching About the Gospel (*2:1-7*)
- True knowledge brings people together in love (*2:1-2*).
- Complete understanding results in seeing God revealed in Christ, who is God (*2:3; see 1 Cor. 1:24, 30*).

"…that their hearts may be encouraged, being knit together in love, and attaining to all riches of the full assurance of understanding, to the knowledge of the mystery of God, both of the Father and of Christ, in whom are hidden all the treasures of wisdom and knowledge" (*2:2-3*).

- Paul warns against false teaching. Even though he is not with the Colossians physically, he wants to see firm faith in them (*2:4-5*).

NOTES

False Teaching and True Correction
False teachers said Christ was only partly God. Paul says Christ was fully God. False teachers said only some people could know the truth. Paul says God's wisdom in Christ is for all people who believe.

- The Christian life is rooted in Christ and continues to grow. All believers live in Christ (*2:6-7*).

4. Christ Is Superior Over False Religions (*2:8-23*)

A. <u>Christ Is Superior Over False Philosophy</u> (*2:8-15*)
- Paul warns against philosophy that does not depend on the truth of Christ (*2:8*).

"For in Him dwells all the fullness of the Godhead bodily; and you are complete in Him, who is the head of all principality and power" (*2:9-10*).

▶ *"Bodily"* — In Christ, God became a man. God is not divided among several spiritual beings (*2:9-10*).

Key Word
Fullness: completeness; nothing is lacking in Christ.

- Paul connects spiritual circumcision and baptism as signs of the work Christ does in bringing new life (*2:11-15*).

"When you were dead in your sins and in the circumcision of your sinful nature, God made you alive with Christ" (*2:13*).

▶ Salvation is not by human ceremonies (*2:11;* see *Deu. 10:16; Rom. 6:6; 7:24*).
▶ Salvation is by the supreme power of God (*2:12, 15;* see *Eph. 1:19-20*).

What is the difference between a teaching that is a different interpretation and a teaching that is false? Discuss.

B. <u>Christ Is Superior Over False Worship</u> (*2:16-19*)
- The ceremonial laws of the Old Testament do not bring salvation. They are only a shadow of the salvation that came in Christ (*2:16*).

"Such a person goes into great detail about what he has seen, and his unspiritual mind puffs him up with idle notions" (*2:18*).

- *"False humility"* — False teachers took pride in humility.
  ▶ They claimed humans must approach God through angels (*2:18*).
  ▶ An *"unspiritual mind"* encourages false worship.

False Teachers and True Correction
False teachers said salvation came through following rituals. Paul says Christ is all we need. False teachers said we must follow rules to avoid sin. Paul says following rules does not control sinful desires.

C. <u>Christ Is Superior Over False Self-denial</u> (*2:20-23*)
- With Christ, believers died to the false teachings of this world. Why should they live by rules about self-denial? (*2:20-21*).

"These things indeed have an appearance of wisdom in self-imposed religion, false humility, and neglect of the body, but are of no value against the indulgence of the flesh" (*2:23*).

- Rules might look like wisdom, but they have no true value (*2:22-23*).
  ▶ False teachers made up rules for Christians to follow.
  ▶ Rules are not bad, but following them does not earn salvation.
  ▶ Following rules is useless to make us not want to sin. Even if we don't sin, we still want to (See *Rom. 7*).

Summarize here the kinds of false teaching Paul corrected.

5. Christ Is Supreme in Christian Living (*3:1–4:6*)

A. <u>Christ Is the Foundation of the Believer's Life</u> (*3:1-4*)
- Paul explains how right teaching leads to right living (*3:1*).
- Believers focus on what is true in heaven, where Christ is (*3:2*).
  ▶ *"Hidden with Christ"* — God has already made our salvation true.
  ▶ Christ is coming again and we will share His glory (*3:3*).

NOTES

NOTES

As you read *chapters 3* and *4*, make two columns. In one column write attitudes and actions Paul says show the "old ways." In the other column write the attitudes and actions that show the "new ways."

Old	New

B. <u>The Believer's Life in Christ Shows a New Nature</u> (*3:5-17*)
- Put aside the old ways that belong to the earthly nature (*3:5-11;* see *2 Cor. 5:7; Rom. 8:9-11*).
    - ▶ Old behaviors: sexual immorality, impurity, lust, evil desires, greed.
    - ▶ All these things deserve the wrath of God.

    "You used to walk in these ways, in the life you once lived. But now you must rid yourself of all such things as these: anger, rage, malice, slander, and filthy language from your lips" (3:7-8).

    - ▶ Paul reminds the Colossians that these things are from the old life.
        - ▷ *"Taken off"* — as if removing soiled clothing.
    - ▶ Believers are renewed in God's image no matter what their background. The church should have no barriers to exclude anyone from God's salvation.
        - ▷ *"Barbarian"* — anyone who did not speak Greek.
        - ▷ *"Schythian"* — known for brutality.
        - ▷ Take on the new ways of Christ (*3:12-14*).
    - ▶ This is a picture of taking off the old clothes and putting on the new clothes (See *Eph. 4:22*).

"Therefore, as God's chosen people, holy and dearly loved, clothe yourselves with compassion, kindness, humility, gentleness and patience" (3:12).

NOTES

- ▶ These new attitudes reflect God's work in people chosen for eternal salvation (See *Gal. 5:22-23*).
- ▶ Remember how much God has forgiven you. Then forgive others (*3:13-14*).

"Over all these virtues put on love, which binds them all together in perfect unity" (3:14).

- Let the peace of Christ rule (*3:15-17*).

"And let the peace of God rule in your hearts, to which also you were called in one body; and be thankful. Let the word of God dwell in you richly in all wisdom, teaching and admonishing one another in psalms, and hymns and spiritual songs, singing with grace in your hearts to the Lord" (3:15-16).

- ▶ Only Christ gives this attitude of peace. We cannot find it elsewhere.
- ▶ *"Rule"* — like an official, as in an athletic game.
- ▶ *"Word of Christ"* — Early Christians had the Old Testament Scriptures only. Additional teachings about Christ were passed orally from person to person (See *Eph. 5:19*).
- ▶ Some important teachings were written as songs in praise of God (See *Eph. 5:14; Phi. 2:6-11; 1 Tim. 3:16*).
- ▶ Honor Christ in all you do (*3:17*).

C. <u>Christ Is Supreme in Relationships</u> (*3:18–4:6*)
  - Family relationships (*3:18-21*).
    - ▶ Husbands and wives.
      - ▷ *"submit"* — a military term that indicates freely yielding to the authority of another person.
      - ▷ Mutual responsibility to submit and love.
    - ▶ Parents and children.
      - ▷ Children obey, and parents treat children with love and respect.
  - Business relationships: masters and slaves (*3:22–4:1*).
    - ▶ Slavery was common at the time, but it is not the main principle of Paul's teaching.
    - ▶ Workers: work as if Christ were your master (*3:23-24*).
    - ▶ Employers: be right and fair (*4:1*).
    - ▶ Paul says more about masters and slaves than about families. This may be because a slave, Onesimus, is going to help deliver the letter (See *4:9* and *Philemon*).

"Whatever you do, do it heartily, as to the Lord and not to men, knowing that from the Lord you will receive the reward of the inheritance; for you serve the Lord Christ" (3:23-24).

NOTES
- Personal relationships (*4:2-6*).
  ▶ Paul encourages prayer and asks for prayer. His prayer is about continuing to proclaim the mystery of Christ (*4:2-3*).
    ▷ He wants to make the mystery clear. This refers again to the theme that Christ is supreme over false religions.
  ▶ Believers should be careful with their public lives.
    ▷ Be ready to share about Christ.

"Walk in wisdom toward those who are outside, redeeming the time. Let your speech always be with grace, seasoned with salt, that you may know how you ought to answer each one" (4:5-6).

    ▷ In speech, use grace as a seasoning, like salt. As salt brings out flavor, gracious speech brings opportunities to talk about Christ. We can do this in appropriate ways.

6. Final Greetings (*4:7-18*)

A. <u>Paul Sends Tychicus and Onesimus with His Letter</u> (*4:7-9*)
   - Tychicus was friend of Paul. He was with Paul for part of his third missionary journey (Act. 20:4).
   - Onesimus was a slave. He ran away from his master in Colosse. He became a Christian in Rome. Paul wrote a separate letter to Philemon.

B. <u>Paul Sends Greetings from People with Him in Rome</u> (*4:10-15*)
   - Aristarchus traveled with Paul on his third missionary journey (*Act. 19:29; 20:4*).
   - Mark traveled with Paul during the second journey. He wrote the Gospel of Mark.
   - Epaphras had started the Colossian church. He had sent a report to Paul.
   - Luke, a doctor, traveled with Paul and is with him in Rome. Luke wrote the Gospel of Luke and the book of Acts.

C. <u>Final instructions</u> (*4:16-18*)
   - Paul asks that his letter be shared with other churches (*4:16*).
   - A special message for Archippus, a fellow worker (*Phm. 2*).
   - Paul's personal signature guaranteed the letter was real.

Suggestions for Preaching From *Colossians*

- Explore these major themes: Christ is God; Christ is the head of the church; believers have union with Christ.

- Explore the false teaching and right corrections that Paul talks about throughout the book. How are these false teachings present today in your country?

- Study how what we believe should affect our actions and relationships.

Chapter Eight
1 Thessalonians

Thessalonica was the capital city of Macedonia. It was on the Egnatian Way. This was the main highway between Rome and eastern parts of the Empire. Paul visited Thessalonica on his second missionary journey. He went to this region because he had a vision from God. In the vision, a man from Macedonia invited Paul to come (See *Act. 16:9-10*). He went first to Philippi, then to Thessalonica.

Paul preached for three Sabbath days in the Jewish synagogue. Most new believers were Gentiles, but Jews also believed. However, some Jews were against Paul. A mob started a riot. They went to the house of Jason, where Paul was staying. When they could not find Paul, they took Jason before the city officials. As a result, the Christians sent Paul and Silas away (See *Act. 17:1-5*).

Paul sent Timothy back to Thessalonica. Timothy brought a report to Paul with questions from the church. Paul wrote *1 Thessalonians* from Corinth around AD 51. The letter talks about many topics, including the Trinity, the deity of Christ, the Scriptures, the Second Coming of Christ and the Resurrection. The letter gave the readers a firm foundation of doctrine. Paul wrote *2 Thessalonians* later that year or the next year. Still, false teaching rose up in the church. In the second letter Paul corrects some wrong teaching about the return of Christ.

Words to watch for:

Key Words: coming, sanctification.

Tip: Open your Bible to *1 Thessalonians* so you can follow the readings.

1. Paul Encourages the Church (*1:1-10*)

A. Greetings for the Church, the Gathering of Believers (*1:1-2*)

B. Thanksgiving for Faithfulness (*1:3-5*)
- *"Work of faith, labor of love, and patience of hope"* —The words *"faith," "love"* and *"hope"* appear together many times in the New Testament (*1:3*; see *Rom. 5:1-5; 1 Cor. 13:13; Gal. 5:5-6; Col. 1:4-5; Heb. 6:10-12; 1 Pet. 1:3-8, 21-22*).
  ▶ Faith leads to action.
  ▶ Hope is firm confidence. Faith produces hope. Hope expects, looks forward to and receives what we believe God promised.
- *"Knowing...your election"* — Paul gives thanks for what God is doing (*1:4-5*).
  ▶ God chose the believers (*1:4*; see *Col. 3:12*).
  ▶ The Gospel comes from God. We preach, but the Holy Spirit changes hearts. The preacher can only preach to the ear. The Holy Spirit must speak to the heart (*1:5*; see *2 Cor. 6:6*).

NOTES

C. <u>Following the Example</u> (*1:6-10*)
- The Thessalonians received the Gospel and followed the example of Paul (*1:6*).
- They became examples themselves. The Gospel spread around the region (*1:7-8*).
- Other people reported to Paul good news about the Thessalonians (*1:9-10*).
  - ▶ *"Turned from idols"* — Most people in the church in Thessalonica were probably Gentiles (*1:9*).
  - ▶ *"Wait for His Son"* — Because of their new faith, they eagerly look forward to the return of Jesus (*1:10;* see *1 The. 1:5; 2 Cor. 7:2*).

2. Paul Explains His Ministry in Thessalonica (*2:1-12*)

A. <u>Paul Wants to Please God, Not Humans</u> (*2:1-4*)
- Some people spoke against Paul after he left (*2:1*).
- The church is proof that the Gospel took hold (*2:2*).
- God gave the Gospel to Paul. Paul gave the same gospel to the Thessalonians (*2:3*).

"But as we have been approved by God to be entrusted with the gospel, even so we speak, not as pleasing men, but God who tests our hearts" (*2:4*).

What does the faith of the Thessalonians tell us about how the Gospel spreads?

B. <u>Paul Points Out the Purpose of His Ministry</u> (*2:5-12*)
- Paul denies that he had wrong motives. He did not preach *"flattering words,"* or seeking *"glory from men."* He asked for nothing (*2:5-6*).
- He preached from love (*2:7-10*).
  - ▶ *"As a nursing mother"* — picture of a mother's tenderness (*2:7-9*).
  - ▶ *"As a father does his own children"* — Paul brought comfort and challenge, as a father does (*2:10-12*).
  - ▶ His actions were blameless. He thought only of the Thessalonians (*2:12;* see *Phil. 1:6; Eph. 4:1; 1 Cor. 1:9*).

"...that you would walk worthy of God who calls you into His own kingdom and glory" (*2:13*).

3. Paul Prays for Spiritual Growth (*2:13–3:13*)

NOTES

A. <u>Concern for Suffering</u> (*2:13-16*)
- The church in Thessalonica began in conflict.
  ▶ Angry men worked against Paul (See *Act. 17:1-15*).
  ▶ Even in the middle of conflict, believers accepted the Gospel (*2:14*).
- Believers in other places suffer too (*2:14-15*).
  ▶ They suffered because they held firm to God's truth (See *1 Pet. 4:16*).
  ▶ In Old Testament history, the people persecuted prophets who spoke the truth.
  ▶ Suffering for Christ should not surprise believers (See *2 Tim. 3:12*).
- Paul suffers too (*2:15-16*).
  ▶ *"Have persecuted us," "forbidding us to speak,"* —Paul himself suffered.
  ▶ *"But wrath has come upon them"* — At the end of time, God will pour out anger on sinful humans.[32]

What encouragement does Paul offer for people who suffer?

B. <u>Paul Wants to Go Back to Thessalonica</u> (*2:17-20*)
- *"Having been taken away"* — This word means a child being separated from a parent. Paul shows his love with this word (*2:17-18*).
- *"Satan stopped us"* — Satan seeks to hinder the spread of the Gospel. We must pray for those preaching God's Word that Satan does not hinder and that doors of opportunity will open (See *1 Cor. 16:9*).
- *"Our hope, or joy, or crown of rejoicing"* — The people in Thessalonica prove that Paul's work for Christ is true.

C. <u>Paul Sends Love through Timothy</u> (*3:1-8*)
- If Paul returned to Thessalonica, trouble would happen. Instead, he sent Timothy, a *"brother and minister of God, and our fellow laborer in the gospel."*
  ▶ Timothy's purpose was to *"establish you"* and *"encourage you."* The Thessalonians have accepted the Gospel. Now they must grow spiritually (*3:1-2*).
- The result will be believers who stand firm in times of trouble (*3:3-5*).
  ▶ *"We told you before…"* — Paul had warned believers that troubles would come (*3:3-4*).
  ▶ *"Tempter," "tempted"* — Satan tempted Jesus (*Mat. 4:1-11*). Now he tempts Christians (*3:5*).
- Timothy's gives his report (*3:6-8*).
  ▶ *"Brought us good news"* — Timothy's report gave comfort to Paul (*3:6-7*).

NOTES

"For now we live, if you stand fast in the Lord" (3:8).

▸ Paul's words show his deep feelings for the new Christians (3:8).

D. Paul Gives the Credit to God (3:9-13)
- Paul did not forget to thank God. He does not take credit for the believers' faith (3:9).
- *"Night and day" "exceedingly"* — frequent prayer. Once again, strong words show strong feelings (3:10).
    ▸ "Perfect what is lacking" — Paul wants to see the believers grow in faith.
- Paul often prays in the middle of a letter (See *Eph. 1:15-23; 3:14-21; Phi. 1:9-11; Col. 1:9-12*).
- Paul's prayer points to God's action.
    ▸ *"May the Lord make you increase and abound"* —Love defines relationships of Christians (3:12).
    ▸ *"So that He may establish"* — holy before God, not just people (3:13).
    ▸ *"Coming of our Lord Jesus Christ"* — the fulfillment of God's plan for salvation (3:13; see *2 The. 2:17*).

Key Word
Coming: The Greek word is *parousia*. It means "presence." In New Testament times, people used the word for a special visit of an important person. New Testament writers use the word to mean Christ's second coming when He returns as King of everything (See *1 The. 3:13; 4:15; 5:23; 2 The. 2:1; 2:8; 2 Pet. 1:16*).[33]

4. Paul Tells Believers to Please God with Their Lives (*4:1-12*)

"Finally then, brethren, we urge and exhort in the Lord Jesus that you should abound more and more, just as you received from us how you ought to walk and to please God" (4:1)

A. Instructions About Morality (4:1-8)
- *"Abstain from sexual immorality"* — In the first century, sexual standards were very low.[34] (See *1 Cor. 5:1; 1 Cor. 5:9-11*).
    ▸ Pagan religions used sexual immorality as a way of worship.
    ▸ Roman culture had few rules about sexual immorality.[35]
- Paul keeps the standard high. God's will is that His people should be holy. They should not have the values of unbelievers.
    ▸ God created the body for a holy purpose (4:7; see *Lev. 11:44*). Sexual relationships outside of marriage dishonor God.

Key Word
Sanctification: The word means "set apart" for God to use. In God's eyes, we are holy because of Christ's sacrifice. At the same time, God keeps on working in us to make us holy (See *Rom. 6:19; Rom. 6:22; 1 Cor. 1:30; 2 Thes. 2:13; Heb. 12:14*).[36]

B. Instructions About Love (4: 9-10)
- *"Love"* — The Greek word is *philadelphia*. In the New Testament it means the love of believers for each other. Jesus commanded Christians to love (See *Joh. 13:34-35; 15:12, 17*).[37]
- Paul urges believers to *"increase more and more"* in love.

C. Instructions About the Christian Life (*4:11-12*)
- *"Quiet life"* — inner peace (*4:11*).
- *"Mind your own business"* — Perhaps people expected Jesus to return soon, so they did not look after their responsibilities (*4:11*).[38]
- *"Work with your own hands"* — Greeks thought work was only for slaves. Christians took work seriously. Some, however, neglected their work (*4:11*).
  - ▶ Paul worked with his hands. He made tents (See *Act. 18:3; 1 The. 2:9*).
  - ▶ The goal in all things is to bring honor to Christ (*4:12*).

D. The Return of Christ (*4:13-18*)
- *"Fallen asleep"* — Some new believers had died already (*4:13*).
- *"Hope"* — Unbelievers fear death. Believers know they will be with God (*4:14*).
- Paul explains what will happen to believers when Christ returns in triumph over sin and death (*4:16*).

"Then we who are alive and remain shall be caught up together with them in the clouds to meet the Lord in the air. And thus we shall always be with the Lord. Therefore comfort one another with these words" (*4:17-18*).

- ▶ Believers who have died will rise from the dead (*4:16*).
- ▶ Believers who are alive will be "caught up" with those who have died. All Christians will meet the Lord in the air (*4:17*).
- ▶ This resurrection is physical (See *1 Cor. 15:51-53; Luk. 24:39; Joh. 20:20, 25, 27*).
- ▶ Resurrection bodies of believers will be like the resurrection body of Christ (See *1 Joh. 3:2*).
- ▶ We will be with the Lord forever (*4:17*; see *Joh. 14:3; 2 Cor. 5:8; Phi. 1:23; Col. 3:4*).

5. The Day of the Lord (*5:1-11*)

A. Teaching About the *"Day of the Lord"* (5:1-3)
- In the Old Testament, the day of the Lord is a time of God's judgment (see *Joe. 1:1-2; Amo. 5:18-20; Zep. 1:14-15*) and rule (*Isa. 2:1-3; Isa. 2:11; Isa. 11:1-9; Isa. 30:23-26; Zec. 14:1; 7-21*).
- Paul uses the phrase to mean the return of Christ and the final judgment.
- The time is uncertain and sudden.
  - ▶ *"As a thief in the night"* (*5:2*).
  - ▶ *"As the labor pains upon a pregnant woman"* (*5:3*).

NOTES

NOTES

B. <u>Unbelievers and Believers Will Have Different Experiences</u> (*5:4-8*)

"You are all sons of light and sons of the day. We are not of the night nor of darkness. Therefore let us not sleep, as others do, but let us watch and be sober" (*5:5-6*).

- *"Of the night,"* *"those who sleep,"* *"drunk at night"* — Unbelievers are not prepared for Christ's coming.
    - ▶ *"Sleep"* — spiritually asleep, rather than dead (See *4:13*, *"fallen asleep"*).
- *"Sons of light,"* *"of the day,"* *"watch and be sober"* — Believers watch and hope for Christ's coming.

"But let us who are of the day be sober, putting on the breastplate of faith and love, and as a helmet the hope of salvation" (*5:8*).

- *"faith,"* *"hope"* and *"love"* appear together again (See *1:3-5*).
- The Day of the Lord brings wrath for unbelievers, but salvation to believers (*5:9-11*).

Why does Paul want believers to know about Christ's return?

How will you preach on the Second Coming of Jesus Christ in your church plant?

6. Paul's Final Instructions (*5:12-28*)

A. <u>Relationship with Leaders</u> (*5:12–13*)
- *"Those who labor among you"* — All the Christians in Thessalonica were new believers.
- Paul teaches believers to honor leaders.

B. <u>Life in the Church Together</u> (*5:14-22*)
- Help each other be faithful (*5:14-16*).
  - ▶ *"Warn those who are unruly"* — *5:14*.
  - ▶ *"Comfort the fainthearted"* — *5:14*.
  - ▶ *"Uphold the weak"* — *5:14*.
  - ▶ *"Be patient with all"* — *5:14*.
- Stay close to God (*5:16-22*).
  - ▶ *"Always"* — joy, prayer and thankfulness do not depend on the Christian's mood. The Spirit works to make us holy in all areas of life (*5:16-18*; see *Phi. 4:4*).[39]
  - ▶ *"Do not quench the Spirit." "Quench"* means to put out a fire (*5:19*).

NOTES

Paul tells believers not to grieve the Holy Spirit (*Eph. 4:30*). We are to walk by the Spirit (*Gal. 5:16*) and be filled (controlled) by the Spirit (*Eph. 5:18*).

  - ▶ *"Test everything."* Right teaching will agree with Paul's teaching (5:20).

Encourage One Another. Read *1 Thessalonians 5:11-23*. How does Paul encourage believers in these verses?

C. <u>Personal Appeals and Blessing</u> (*5:23-28*)

"Now may the God of peace Himself sanctify you completely; and may your whole spirit, soul and body be preserved blameless at the coming of our Lord Jesus Christ. He who calls you is faithful, who also will do it" (*5:23-24*).

- Paul sums up his theme of sanctification.
  - ▶ God wants every part of the believer's life to show they are dedicated to God.
  - ▶ We are to Show holiness in actions so Christ will approve when He returns.
- *"Holy kiss"* — This may have been a customary greeting.
- Paul reminds readers that Christians are saved by grace and live by grace (*5:28*).[40]

NOTES **Suggestions for Preaching from *1 Thessalonians***

- Study the theme of persecution in *1 Thessalonians*. How does the Holy Spirit help believers stay strong?

- Explore the theme of how the Christian's life now is related to the future.

- Study the theme of encouragement in *chapter 5*.

- Encourage your family, your new congregation and lift up other church planters you know in prayer. They each need your positive words.

Chapter Nine
2 Thessalonians

Paul wrote *2 Thessalonians* later in the same year he wrote *1 Thessalonians*, or the next year. False teaching was still a problem in the church. In this letter Paul corrects some wrong teaching about the return of Christ.

What to watch for:

Key Word: lawless one.

Tip: Open your Bible to *2 Thessalonians* so you can follow the readings.

1. Faithfulness in Persecution (*1:1-12*)

   A. Greeting (*1:1-2*)

   B. The Thessalonians Had Been Faithful (*1:3-5*)
   - *"Faith grows exceedingly"* — Even in persecution, the Christians in Thessalonica grew in faith.
   - *"Counted worthy of the kingdom of God"* — If believers respond to troubles in the right way, God will consider them worthy of great reward (*1:5;* see *Mat. 5:12; 1 Pet. 2:19*).

   C. Suffering Shows the Justice of God (*1:6-10*)
   - *"Repay with tribulation"* — God's judgment means those who are not righteous will be punished (*1:6;* see *Psa. 9, 10, 17, 137; Rev. 6:9-10*).
   - When Christ returns, He will free Christians from suffering. This gives hope in suffering (*1:7-10*).
     - ▶ "Revealed from heaven" — Now Christ is at the right hand of God in heaven (*1:7;* see *Jude 14*).
     - ▶ One day He will return to earth in a visible way (*1:7-8*).
     - ▶ God will be the judge of people who reject Christ and bring glory to those who accept Christ (*1:9-10;* see *Phi. 3:19*).

   D. Paul Prays for Spiritual Progress (*1:11-12*)
   - *"That God may count you worthy of his calling"* — Paul always points believers to their true purpose. God is at work in their lives to bring glory to Jesus (*1:11*).
   - *"Name"* — In ancient cultures, a person's name summed up the person. Bringing glory to Christ's name means bringing glory to Christ (*1:12;* see *Col. 3:17*).[41]

2. Teaching on the Day of the Lord (2:1-17)

A. <u>False Teachers</u> (*2:1-2*)

"Now, brethren, concerning the coming of our Lord Jesus Christ and our gathering together to Him, we ask you, not to be soon shaken in mind or troubled, either by spirit or by word or by letter, as if from us, as though the day of Christ had come" (*2:1-2*).

- After Paul wrote *1 Thessalonians*, he heard some teachers said the *"Day of the Lord"* had begun (*2:1-2*).
- Some believers thought the Second Coming of Jesus had happened already. They were surprised because they understood different things would occur if the day of the Lord had come. When these things were not occurring, they became vulnerable to the false teaching.

B. <u>Paul's Teaching</u> (*2:3-17*)

"For the mystery of the lawlessness is already at work; only He who retrains will do so until He is taken out of the way. And then the lawless one will be revealed" (*2:7-8*)

- Paul says the *"Day of the Lord"* has not come yet.

- *"Falling away," "man of sin"* — A great rebellion will happen before the Second Coming (*2:3-4*; see *1 Tim. 4:1; Joh. 17:2*).
- Evil is at work in the world but not at full power. This is the *"mystery of lawlessness"* (*2:7*).
- *"Restraining"* — Paul does not clearly identify the one who holds back the rebellion (*2:6-7*).
  - ▶ The restrainer may be the Roman Empire, Paul's missionary work, the Jewish nation, law and government, or the Holy Spirit.[42]
  - ▶ *"Taken out of the way"* (*2:7*).
    - ▷ Some see this as the "Rapture." If the church is not on earth, nothing will hold back the rebellion (See *1 The. 5:16-17*). If this is the Rapture, then the Restrainer would probably be the Holy Spirit.

Key Word
Lawless One: The word means "without law." The "lawless one" is the same as the "Antichrist" (*1 Joh. 4:2-3*) and the "beast" (*Rev. 13:1*). The lawless one rebels against God and works against Christ's kingdom (See *2 The. 2:8; 1 Tim. 1:9; 2 Pet. 2:8*).[43]

- When the great rebellion happens, Christ will triumph over evil (*2:8*).
- Satan is the power behind the "lawless one." He is powerful, but Christ is more powerful (*2:8-9*).

Paul preached that we have salvation through Christ's death. Why does he also stress that Christ will come again?

NOTES

- *"for this reason"* — Rejecting the truth leads to a judgment of "guilty" (*2:11-12;* see *Rom. 1:28*).

C. <u>God Works in Believers</u> (*2:13-17*)
- It is important to believe the truth.
  ▶ God saves people who believe in Him. Then believers respond to His work. God makes them holy by His Spirit (*2:13-14;* see *Col. 3:12; 1 The. 1:4; Eph. 4:25-28*).
    ▷ Paul assures these people that they have not been left behind. God has always had plans for them. These verses show the beauty of how God has chosen *the ends and the means* of His people's salvation. God chose His elect from the foundation of the world. In time the Holy Spirit set them apart through His work of sanctification. This produces a response to the truth of the Gospel as it is used to call out to His people.
    ▷ Ultimately the believers will be glorified. The believers must believe the truth, the witnesses must preach the truth, and God will call out His people. Nowhere does the Bible teach that the elect will be saved without believing or without someone bringing them the Gospel.
  ▶ *"Tradition"* — the truth that God has revealed in the Gospel. This is the same truth Paul preached to the Thessalonians (*2:15*).
- God Himself gives the inner strength believers need (*2:16-17*).

3. Continue to Be Faithful (*3:1-15*)

A. <u>Paul Asks for Prayer</u> (*3:1-5*)
- Paul prays for the work of the Gospel (*3:1-2*).
- *"The Lord is faithful"* — Paul's confidence is in the Lord (*3:3-5*).

"Now may the Lord direct your hearts into the love of God and into the patience of Christ" (*3:5*).

B. <u>Paul Condemns Idleness</u> (*3:6-15*)
- Paul has already warned against idleness in (See *1 The. 4:11-12; 5:14*).
  ▶ Some believers may have thought they did not have to work because Christ would come soon.
  ▶ The problem was bad enough that Paul has to write about it again (*3:6-10*).
- Paul urges the people to follow his example.

- Here is a challenge to the church people to follow the godly example of the leaders.
- It also is a challenge to the leaders to be worthy of following.
- Those who do not work cause division in the church (*3:11-13*).

"For even when we were with you, we commanded you this: If anyone will not work, neither shall he eat. For we hear that there are some among you who walk in a disorderly manner, not working at all, but are busybodies" (*3:10-11*).

- *"Do not keep company"* — Paul says to withdraw from a person who does not obey (*3:14-15*).

4. A Blessing of Grace and Peace (*3:16-18*)

Suggestions for Preaching From *2 Thessalonians*

- Study what Paul says about Christ's Second Coming.

- How does the hope of Christ's return affect our lives now?

- This Blessed Hope is given along with all of eschatology to cause us to live a pure life in Jesus Christ. He is concerned about holy living and this compels us even more to live in His Spirit.

CHAPTER TEN
PHILEMON

Philemon was a slave-owner. Onesimus was his slave. They may have lived in Colosse, one of the cities in Asia Minor. This is modern-day Turkey. Philemon was a Christian. Onesimus ran away from his owner and found Paul. By this time, Paul was a prisoner in Rome. Under Roman law, a runaway slave could be put to death. Paul still believed Onesimus should return to Philemon. Paul wrote this letter to ask Philemon to receive Onesimus as a brother in Christ, not just a slave. This is not a letter to a church, but a personal letter.

Tip: Open your Bible to *Philemon* so you can follow the readings.

1. Greetings and Prayer (*1-7*)

    A. <u>Paul Greets Philemon in a Personal Way</u> (*1-3*)
- Philemon is a "friend" and "fellow worker" (*1*).
- Paul names others in the church (*2*).
  ▶ Apphia may have been Philemon's wife.
  ▶ Archippus may have been the pastor of the church in Colosse.[44] (See *Col. 4:17;* Archippus was in Colosse).

    B. <u>Paul Shows Affection for Philemon</u> (*4-7*)
- Paul has received good reports about Philemon (*5*).
- Paul prays for Philemon (*4, 6*).

> "...that the sharing of your faith may become effective by the acknowledgement of every good thing which is in you in Christ Jesus" (*6*).

- Philemon's love has encouraged and refreshed Paul (*7*).

2. Paul's Plea with Philemon to Take the Slave Back (*8-22*)

    A. <u>Paul Makes a Personal Appeal</u> (*8-9*)
- Paul could have commanded Philemon to take back Onesimus because Paul was an apostle (*8*).
- Rather than use his authority, Paul asks for love (*9*).
  ▶ *"The aged"* — Paul may be speaking of his age. This letter was written late in his ministry. It may also refer to Paul's being an elder.

    B. <u>Paul Speaks of Onesimus</u> (*10-11*)
- *"My son"* — the idea of father and child (*10;* see *1 Tim. 1:2; Tit 1:4*).
- *"While in my chains"* — as a prisoner in Rome, Paul introduced Onesimus to Christ (*10*).
- *"Profitable"* — this word is a play on words because the name Onesimus means "useful." Onesimus had not been useful to Philemon in the past. Now he is useful to both Paul and Philemon (*11*).

NOTES

C. Paul Explains Why He Sends Onesimus Back (*12-14*)
- *"I am sending him back"* — Onesimus belongs to Philemon, so Paul sends the slave back. Philemon can decide what to do (*12, 14*).
- *"Consent"* — Philemon might agree that Onesimus should help Paul in Rome, but the owner must make the decision (*13-14*).
  ▶ Paul does not force Philemon's decision.
  ▶ Serving is voluntary.

> *"You therefore receive him, that is, my own heart, whom I wished to keep with me, that on your behalf he might minister to me in my chains for the gospel"* (*12-13*)

D. Onesimus's Running Away May Have a Purpose (*15-16*)
- *"Separated"* — The separation changed Onesimus. He became a Christian. He can return to Philemon ready to serve (*15*).
- *"Brother"* — Philemon and Onesimus are no longer just master and slave. They are now brothers in the Lord (*16*).

E. Paul's Plea (*17-22*)
- *"Partner"* — Philemon should receive Onesimus as he would receive Paul himself (*17*).
- *"Owes"* — Onesimus may have stolen from Philemon (*18-19*).
  ▶ Because he writes with his own hand, Paul takes on the debt in a legal document.[45]
  ▶ Paul reminds Philemon of his own debt to Paul for leading him to Christ.
- *"Confidence in your obedience"* — Paul expects Philemon will do as he asks and will even welcome Paul later.

F. Blessing (*23-25*)
- Paul closes with personal greetings, as he always does (*23-24*).
- The blessing of God's grace begins and ends this letter (*3, 25*).

What lessons does this letter teach on forgiveness and acceptance?

Suggestions for Preaching From *Philemon*

- Explore barriers that get in the way of Christian unity.

- Teach the lessons this story explains about forgiveness and respect.

Chapter Eleven
Hebrews

The book of *Hebrews* is a mystery. We cannot be sure who wrote it. We cannot be sure who first read it. We cannot be sure when it was written. Yet, *Hebrews* is a major book in the New Testament.

Hebrews was written before the Jewish temple was destroyed in AD 70. The author speaks of the work of priests in the present tense. Most scholars believe the first readers were Jewish Christians. *Hebrews* uses many Old Testament passages and talks about many Jewish themes. The phrase "they who are from Italy" (*13:24*) may mean people in Italy or from Italy. The readers may have been Jewish Christians living in Rome. They had many questions about the temple and the law of Moses for Christians. Some wondered if Jesus really was better than the Jewish system.

The theme of *Hebrews* is that Jesus Christ holds the highest place in God's plan for salvation. Jesus is the final revelation. He is the last word. He is the final sacrifice. The Jewish Scriptures explained the "old covenant." Jesus Christ brings the "new covenant." The new covenant is better than the old covenant. Christians should not give up on salvation through Christ.

***Hebrews* describes the qualities and actions of Christ. The following 10 passages are important to understanding the full picture of Christ:**

1. *1:1-4* — "Heir of all things," "the One through whom God made the worlds," "brightness of God's glory," "express image of His person," "upholding all things by the word of his power," "seated at the right hand of the Majesty on high," "better than the angels."
2. *2:10* — Captain of salvation.
3. *2:14* — Destroyer of the devil.
4. *2:17* — Faithful High Priest.
5. *3:3* — Worthy of more glory than Moses.
6. *4:15* — A High Priest who knows our weakness.
7. *7:25* — Intercedes.
8. *8:6* — Mediator of a new covenant.
9. *12:2-3* — Model for enduring troubles from sinners.
10. *13:20* — Great Shepherd.[46]

***Hebrews* contains six important warnings or words of advice:**

1. Warning against drifting from the truth we have heard (*2:1-4*).
2. Warning against disbelieving the voice of God (*3:7-14*).
3. Warning against falling away from the elementary principle of Christ (*5:11-6:20*).
4. Warning against despising the knowledge of the truth (*10:26-39*).
5. Warning about the grace of God being devalued (*12:25-29*).
6. Warning not to depart from Him "who speaks" (*12:25-29*).

NOTES

What to watch for:

Key words: more excellent, high priest, mercy/grace, Melchizedek, eternal, faith, covenant.

Tip: Open your Bible to *Hebrews* so you can follow the readings.

1. Christ Is God's Final Word (*1:1-4*)

"God, who at various times and in various ways spoke in time past to the fathers by the prophets, has in these last days spoken to us by His Son" (1:1-2).

A. <u>God Speaks in a New Way</u> (*1:1-2*)
- *"In time past," "in these last days"* — All Old Testament writers are "prophets" in this setting. Now God speaks by His Son (*1:1-2*).
- *"Heir of all things," "made the worlds"* — Christ was present at creation. He is the Son of God Himself (*1:2*).

B. <u>Christ Is a Better Way for God to Speak</u> (*1:3-4*)
- *"Brightness of God's glory"* — We cannot separate the brightness of Christ from the brightness of God (*1:3*).
- *"Right hand of the Majesty on high"* — Christ sits at God's right hand. This means He is ruling with God. He is Lord over all (*1:4;* see *Heb. 1:13; 8:1; 10:12; 12:2; Mat. 26:64; Act. 2:23; 5:34; Rom. 8:34; Eph. 1:20; Col. 3:1; 1 Pet. 3:22*).

2. Christ is a Superior Person (*1:5–6:20*)

A. <u>Christ Is Better Than Angels</u> (*1:5–2:18*)
- Christ is God's Son. The place of honor belongs to Christ (*1:5-14*).
  - ▶ God speaks of Christ in a way He does not speak of angels (*1:5*).
  - ▶ The writer uses Old Testament passages to show that Christ is better than the angels (See *Psa. 2:7; 2 Sam. 7:14; Deu. 32:43; Psa. 104:4; Psa. 45:6-7; Isa. 61:1; Isa. 61:3; Isa. 50:9; Isa. 51:6*).
    - ▷ Angels are "sons of God," but they are never the "Son of God" (*1:5-6*).
    - ▷ The angels serve Christ (*1:7*).
    - ▷ Christ sits on an eternal throne (*1:8-9*).
    - ▷ Christ is the Creator (*1:10-11*).
    - ▷ The angels serve. Christ rules (*1:13-14*). God sends angels to serve God's people - *"the heirs of salvation."*

Key Word
More Excellent: The writer uses words for "better" or "more excellent" 15 times in the book of Hebrews. A major theme is to show how Christ is better than the ways God spoke in the past.[47]

- Word of advice: Pay attention to salvation (*2:1-4*).
  - ▶ This is the first of five words of advice, or warnings, for the Christian to focus on the Gospel (For the other four, see *3:7-4:13; 6:4-8; 10:26-31; 12:25-29*).

  "Therefore we must give the more earnest heed to the things we have heard, lest we drift away" (*2:1*).

  - ▶ *"Drift away"* — carried away by opinions not based on the Word of God (*2:1*).
  - ▶ *"Spoken through angels"* — God used angels to call Moses (*2:2-3*; see *Exo. 3:2*).
    - ▷ The Gospel is greater than the law.
    - ▷ Disobeying the law brought punishment. Rejecting the Gospel will bring greater punishment.

Reading *Hebrews 2:3*, how do we ignore or neglect this Great Salvation?

Why is this Salvation So Great?

Summarize how Christ is better than angels.

  - ▶ God confirmed the Gospel message through miracles (*2:4*).
- Christ is the perfect Man (*2:5-18*).
  - ▶ The author explores *Psa. 8:4-6* to show that Christ is better than the angels.

  "For in that He put all in subjection under him, He left nothing that is not put under him. But now we do not yet see all things put under him" (*2:8*).

NOTES

- Christ was made *"lower than the angels"* (*2:5-9*).
  - In creation God gave humans authority over other creatures.
  - Christ became human.
- God puts everything under the authority of Christ. This includes angels (*2:8*).
  - Because Christ was human, He could get back the authority humans lost because of sin.
  - Christ holds a position of honor. His death and resurrection bring salvation.
- Because He was made like us, He could save us (*2:10-18*).

"For it was fitting for Him, for whom are all things and by whom are all things, in bringing many sons to glory, to make the captain of their salvation perfect through sufferings. For both He who sanctifies and those who are being sanctified are all one, for which reason He is not ashamed to call them brethren" (*2:10-11*).

- *"captain"* — This means "the first one to lead the way." Jesus went through suffering and became the perfect leader. The word may also be translated "author" or "founder."
- The author uses more Old Testament verses (*2:12-13*; see *Psa. 22:22, 2 Sam. 22:3, Isa. 8:18*).
- *"so that by his death"* — (*2:14*). Because Jesus became flesh and died on the cross, He defeated the devil's power of death over believers. Man is fallen in his sin and Satan is the accuser of people when they sin and demands that they die for their sin. However, Christ died for the sins of the believer so that those sins have no more power of death over the Christians. Therefore Satan's accusations hold no power or fear over us (*Col. 2:14-15*).

"Therefore in all things He had to be made like His brethren, that He might be a merciful and faithful High Priest in things pertaining to God, to make propitiation for the sins of the people" (*2:17*).

- *"make propitiation"* — sacrifice to satisfy God's holiness. Jesus was without sin, but he died on the cross as a sacrifice for us (*2:17*).
- Because Jesus suffered, He is able to help us when we suffer (*2:18*).

B. <u>Christ Is Better Than Moses</u> (*3:1–4:13*)
  - Christ is a Son. Moses is a servant (*3:1-6*).
    - *"In all His house"* — the tabernacle where Israel worshipped. Moses was faithful when he obeyed God's instructions (*3:1*; see *Num. 12:7*).

"For this One has been counted worthy of more glory than Moses, inasmuch as He who built the house has more honor than the house. For every house is built by someone, but He who built all things is God" (*3:3-4*).

  - Christ was faithful when He obeyed the Father. God made a new house—the church.[48]

"And Moses indeed was faithful in all His house as a servant, for a testimony of those things which would be spoken afterward, but Christ as a Son over His own house, whose house we are if we hold fast the confidence and rejoicing of the hope firm to the end" (3:5-6).

- ▶ God's people make up the house God built (*3:6;* see *Eph. 2:19; 1 Pet. 2:5*).

Summarize how Christ is better than Moses.

- Word of advice: Trust the Word; do not doubt (*3:7–4:13*).
  - ▶ This section is based on *Psa. 95:7-11*.
  - ▶ *Psa. 95* summarizes the history of Israel under Moses as a leader in the desert.
    - ▷ *"trial in the wilderness"* — the years Moses led the Israelites in the wilderness (See *Exo. 17:1-7*).
    - ▷ *"rest"* — key concept in Hebrews. The Old Testament speaks of "rest" victory in the Promised Land (See *Deu. 3:20; 12:9; 25:19; Jos. 11:23; 21:44; 22:4; 23:1*). The New Testament speaks of "rest" as the believer's eternal home.[49]

  "Beware, brethren, lest there be in any of you an evil heart of unbelief in departing from the living God; but exhort one another daily, while it is called 'Today,' lest any of you be hardened through the deceitfulness of sin" (3:12-13).

  - ▶ *"Departing from the living God"* — active rebellion against God (*3:12*).
    - ▷ See *Num. 14:1-3*. The Israelites gave up hoping in God.
  - ▶ *"Exhort one another"* — believers share responsibility to encourage one another (*3:13*).
  - ▶ *"Partakers of Christ"* — sharing with Christ in the heavenly kingdom. The Israelites started well, but later doubted.[50]
    - ▷ People who did not enter the Promised Land were people who heard God's promise and did not believe. God kept the whole generation out of the land (See *Num. 14:21-35*).
    - ▷ Jewish Christians considered returning to the Jewish system, rather than believing in Jesus.
  - ▶ The writer to the Hebrews warns those who have heard the Gospel and God's Word over and over again, yet have not acted on it. Every time a person hears the truth of God's Word and chooses not to obey, that person or church acts in unbelief. These same people were having their spiritual hearts hardened. This is a process that is subtle and deadly.

NOTES

- ▷ A Valuable Privilege (*3:7*). The *inspiration* and *illumination* of the *"Holy Spirit says ..."*
- ▷ A Scary Process (*3:8, 13*). The issue of *"hardened hearts of unbelief." "Deceitfulness of sin"* — sin pulls people in with the promise that disobedience is more secure (*Exo. 17:3*), and more pleasurable (*Heb. 11:25-26; Exo. 16:3*) than a walk of faith with the Lord.
- ▷ A Provocative People (*3:8-11*). The *illustration* of "your fathers" (Israel).
- ▷ A Positive Persuasion (*3:13*). The *influence* of an "exhorting" church.
- ▷ A Personal Plea (*3:7, 13, 15*). The *invitation* is for "TODAY, if YOU will hear."
- ▷ A Persistent Partaker (*3:14*). The *indication* of a true believer.

"Therefore, since the promise of entering his rest still stands, let us be careful that none of you be found to have fallen short of it" (4:1).

▶ The tragedy of the Israelites in the desert is a warning for believers.
▶ *"The promise of rest still stands"* — God still keeps His promise to His people (*4:1*).
  - ▷ God made a covenant promise to Abraham to send a Messiah (See *Gen. 15:12-21; 17:1-8; 22:15-18*).
  - ▷ God repeated His promise through David (See *2 Sam. 7:5-16*).
  - ▷ Through David, God kept His promise to send a Messiah (See *Isa. 11:1-9*).
  - ▷ In Jesus, God kept His promise.
  - ▷ When Christ comes again, God's people will enter His rest (See *Isa. 65:17; 66:22; Rev. 21:4*).[51]
▶ The Israelites did not enter the "rest" of the Promised Land because they did not have faith in the promise. The readers of Hebrews also struggled to have faith (*4:2-6*).
  - ▷ *"God rested"* — The theme of rest goes back to the creation (*4:4; see Gen. 2:2*).

"For if Joshua had given them rest, then He would not afterward have spoken of another day. There remains therefore a rest for the people of God" (4:8-9).

▶ Joshua led God's people into the Promised Land. This was only part of what it means to enter God's rest.
  - ▷ God spoke later, in the time of David, of *"another day."* (*Psa. 95:7-8*).
  - ▷ A Sabbath rest "remains" for God's people in the future (*4:9*).

"Let us therefore be diligent to enter that rest, lest anyone should fall according to the same example of disobedience" (4:11).

  - ▷ *"Word of God"* — God's message is still active (*4:13*) It shows the sinful parts of a believer's heart.

>   ▷ God sees everything in our hearts.
>   ▶ The purpose of this "word of advice" is to encourage believers to stand firm in their faith. They have heard the Gospel and should keep following it.

C. Christ Is Better Than the Priesthood of Aaron (*4:14–5:11*)
   • Jesus is the High Priest (4:14-16).

Key Word
High Priest: The high priest was the highest religious leader in Israel. Israel went to the high priest to find the will of God. The high priest made offerings for the sin of all the people (*Lev. 4:3-21*). On the Day of Atonement, the high priest entered the Holy Place in the temple. No one else could go in. He sprinkled blood on the mercy seat.[52]

>   ▶ In the Old Testament, the high priest went into the Most Holy Place on the Day of Atonement. Jesus went into the heavenly sanctuary when he finished His work of atonement (*4:14; see Lev. 16:15-17; Act. 1:9-11*).
>   ▶ *"Sympathize with our weaknesses"* — Jesus was human and knows our suffering (*4:15*).

"Let us therefore come boldly to the throne of grace, that we may obtain mercy and find grace to help in time of need" (*4:16*)

>   ▶ Because Christ did the work of a priest, believers can come near to God.
> • Jesus is qualified to be the High Priest (*5:1-10*).
>   ▶ In the Old Testament, the high priest must be a person God calls. No one chooses for himself to be the high priest (*5:1-4*).
>   ▷ *"gifts and sacrifices"* — the work of the high priest on the Day of Atonement.
>   ▷ *"for his own sin"* — the high priest was sinful, as were all the people.
>   ▷ Aaron was the brother of Moses. He was the beginning of the line of priests.
>   ▶ God called Christ to be the High Priest (*5:5*).

"So also Christ did not glorify Himself to become High Priest, but it was He who said to him" (*5:5*).

>   ▷ Christ was human, and God called Him. He was qualified to be High Priest.
>   ▶ *"Learned obedience"* — Jesus obeyed God's will. The high priest in the Old Testament sacrificed an animal. Jesus sacrificed Himself (*5:8*).
>   ▶ *"Having been perfected"* — Jesus was perfect. "Perfected" means he carried out God's plan (*5:9*).
>   ▶ *"Source of eternal salvation"* — Because Jesus carried out God's plan, we have salvation. Christ's sacrifice is the final sacrifice. We no longer need the Jewish system of sacrifice (*5:9; see Heb. 2:10*).

NOTES   **Summarize how Christ is better than the priests of Aaron's line.**

Key Word
Mercy/Grace: The words "mercy" and "grace" often appear together in the New Testament (See *Eph. 2:4-5; 1 Tim. 1:2; 1 Pet. 1:2-3*). "Mercy" is God actively helping those in need. "Grace" is God's tendency to treat us with kindness we don't deserve. The Old Testament uses a Hebrew word which means "loving-kindness." Christ shows us God's grace and mercy. Both are gifts from God.

- Word of advice: Don't become dull. Press on to spiritual maturity (*5:11–6:12*).
  ▶ The writer scolds the readers for being immature (*5:12-6:3*).

  "For though by this time you ought to be teachers, you need someone to teach you again the first principles of the oracles of God; and you have come to need milk and not solid food. For everyone who partakes only of milk is unskilled in the word of righteousness for he is a babe" (5:12-13).

   ▷ *"first principles"* — This phrase refers to simple letters or numbers. It means basic truths (*5:12*).
   ▷ *"unskilled"* — The readers had information, but their actions did not match up (*5:13*).
   ▷ *"full age"* — the mature believer (*5:14*).
   ▷ *"elementary principles of Christ"* — truths the readers had learned already (*6:1*).
   ▷ *"eternal judgment"* — God will judge everyone (*6:2*; see *1 Cor. 3:12-15; Rev. 20:11-15*).
   ▷ The milk here is all of the Word of God. The meat is the practice of the Word of God. They understood deep doctrines (milk) but were not practicing them (meat).
  ▶ The readers have not been growing spiritually (*6:4-8*).

  "For it is impossible for those who were once enlightened, and have tasted the heavenly gift and have become partakers of the Holy Spirit, and have tasted the good word of God and the powers of the age to come, if they fall away, to renew them again to repentance, since they crucify again for themselves the Son of God, and put Him to an open shame" (6:4-6).

   ▷ Some believe this passage means true Christians will never "fall away." People may seem to believe but not truly believe (See *Joh. 6:39-40; 10:27-29; Rom. 8:28-30*).
   ▷ Others believe this passage means Christians who stop believing (See *2 Cor. 11:1-4, 13-15; 2 Tim. 2:17-18; 1 Joh. 2:21-25*).

▷ Remember the context. Most likely these verses talk about Jewish believers who face temptation to go back to Jewish ways. It means falling away from spiritual maturity.⁵³
▷ The way in which the verses are written here support that these were believers, who were struggling spiritually with the persecution these Jewish Christians faced. We can feel for them and for many today who face the same.
▶ The writer is sure God is working (*6:9-12*).

"But, beloved, we are confident of better things concerning you, yes, things that accompany salvation" (6:9).
▷ The good works of the readers were signs that their faith was real (*6:9*).
▷ *"Sluggish"* — This is the same as "dull" in *5:11*.
• God will keep His promise (*6:13-20*).
▶ *"God made a promise to Abraham"* — Abraham's faith is an example. He believed God's promise (*6:12-15*; see *Gen. 12:3-4; 17:2; 18:10; 21:5*).
▶ *"Confirmation"* — a guarantee (*6:16-17*).
▶ *"Two immutable things"* — The first is God's promise, which does not change, and the second is God's oath, which does not change (*6:18*).

"This hope we have as an anchor of the soul, both sure and steadfast, and which enters the Presence beyond the veil, where the forerunner has entered for us, even Jesus, having become the High Priest forever according to the order of Melchizedek" (6:19-20).

▶ *"Anchor"* — Hope in Christ holds us firmly in place as an anchor holds a ship (*6:19*).
▶ *"Beyond the veil"* — The most holy place in the Jewish temple where God lives. As high priest, Christ goes before believers to God (*6:19*; see *Lev. 16:2, 15*).
▶ *"Forerunner"* — Jesus goes first to the presence of God. Believers follow (*6:20*).

3. Christ Is a Better Priesthood (*7:1–10:19*)

A. <u>A Better Line of Priests</u> (*7:1-25*)
• The priesthood of Melchizedek is better than the line of priests from Aaron (*7:1-10*).
▶ *"Without father, without mother"* — The Bible gives no record of Melchizedek's birth or death. Melchizedek points to Christ, the eternal priest (*7:3*).

"Now consider how great this man was, to whom even the patriarch Abraham gave a tenth of the spoils" (7:4).

▶ *"Patriarch"* — shows that Abraham was great. Melchizedek was greater.

NOTES

- ▶ *"The lesser is blessed by the better"* — The one who receives the tithe is greater than the one who gives the tithe (*7:7*).
- ▶ *"Paid tithes through Abraham"* — The people of Israel came from Abraham. Because he paid tithes to Melchizedek, all the priests paid these tithes (*7:6-9*).
- ▶ Melchizedek was better than Abraham. He was also better than the Old Testament priests.

Key Word

Melchizedek: The Old Testament talks about Melchizedek in the story of Abraham (*Gen. 14:18-20*) and a song of David (*Psa. 110:4*). He was a king of Jerusalem. He blessed Abraham in the name of the true God and Abraham gave him a tithe offering. This meant Abraham believed Melchizedek was a priest of the true God. Like Melchizedek, Jesus was and is both King and Priest.

- • Christ replaces the priesthood of Aaron (*7:11-19*).
  - ▶ God set up the Jewish priesthood from the tribe of Levi. Why do we need a new priesthood?
    - ▷ The law of Moses and the priesthood went together. All people were sinners. They needed a priest to make a sacrifice for their sins.
    - ▷ The Levitical priesthood (priests of Aaron) were not able to make the people holy. No one can be made righteous by following the law.
    - ▷ David announced a new priesthood was coming (*7:11*; see *Psa. 110:4*).
    - ▷ *"The order of Melchizedek"* — The new priesthood would be forever.
  - ▶ If the priesthood changes, the law changes (*7:12*).

  "For the priesthood being changed, of necessity there is also a change of the law" (*7:13*).

    - ▷ The new priesthood did not come from the line of Aaron or the tribe of Levi.
    - ▷ The believer is not under the law of Moses. Instead, Christ makes us righteous (See *Rom. 6:14; Gal. 3:24-25*).
  - ▶ *"He of whom these things are spoken"* — Christ, who came from the tribe of Judah. Christ is not under the law (*7:13-15*).
  - ▶ The new priesthood is eternal (*7:17-19*).

  "For He testifies: 'You are a priest forever according to the order of Melchizedek'" (*7:17*).

    - ▷ *"annulling"* — putting away. Jesus is a new kind of Priest. The law is changed (*7:18*).
    - ▷ The law never made anything perfect. The law only prepared the way for Christ (*7:19*; see *Mat. 5:17; Gal. 3:23-24*).
- • Christ is the true Priest (*7:21-28*).
  - ▶ God gave an oath (*7:20-21*; see *Psa. 110:4*).

"And inasmuch as He was not made priest without an oath (for they have come priests without an oath, but He with an oath by Him who said to Him, "The Lord has sworn And will not relent 'You are a priest forever According to the order of Melchizedek'" (7:20-21).

NOTES

- ▷ An oath was a guarantee (See *6:17*).
- ▷ The oath guarantees a better covenant (See *chapters 8–10*).
- ▶ Christ's priesthood does not change (*7:23-25*).
  - ▷ In the Levitical priesthood, the high priest changed when one died.[54]
  - ▷ *"save to the uttermost"* — save completely.
  - ▷ *"always lives to make intercession"* — Jesus pleads for us.
  - ▷ Christ's ministry of saving and interceding are based on a permanent priesthood (*7:25;* see *1 Joh. 2:2-2; Joh. 17:6-26*).

Summarize how Christ's priesthood is better than the Old Testament priesthood.

Key Word
Eternal: The writer of *Hebrews* stresses that Christ's work is permanent. Jesus is the author of eternal salvation (*5:9*). He obtained eternal salvation (*9:12*), and shares the promise of eternal inheritance (*9:15;* see also *1:8; 5:6; 6:20; 7:17; 7:21; 13:8*).

Jesus the High Priest in *Hebrews*
- He was qualified (*2:11-18*).
- He knows our weakness (*4:15*).
- God called him (*5:5*).
- He was like Melchizedek, not Aaron (*5:10*).
- He had no sin (*7:27-28*).
- He gave himself as the final sacrifice (*8:26; 10:10*).
- His priesthood is eternal (*7:25*).

B. <u>Christ Brings a Better Covenant</u> (*8:1-13*)
- Christ's work is in heaven, not on earth (*8:1-6*).

"Now this is the main point of the things we are saying: We have such a High Priest, who is seated at the right hand of the throne of the Majesty in the heavens, a Minister of the sanctuary and of the true tabernacle which the Lord erected, and not man" (8:1-2).

- ▶ *"Tabernacle"* — In Israel's early history, the people worshiped in a tent.
  - ▷ God lived in the Most Holy place of the tabernacle.
  - ▷ In later history, Israel had a temple building. God was still in the Most Holy place.

NOTES

- ▷ In the tabernacle of Moses, the high priest went to the Most Holy place only one time a year.
- ▷ In the tabernacle of heaven, the high priest is with God all the time.
- ▶ *"Who serve"* — The present tense shows that the Jewish temple was still standing when Hebrews was written (*8:4*).
- ▶ The earthly priesthood and the earthly tabernacle were shadows of what is in heaven (*8:4*).
    - ▷ God gave Moses clear instructions (*8:5; see Exo. 25:40*).
    - ▷ The tabernacle was a symbol of how humans came to a holy God (*8:6*).
- ▶ Christ brings humans to God in a better covenant (*8:6*).
• The new covenant is better than the old covenant (*8:7-9*).

"For if that first covenant had been faultless, then no place would have been sought for a second" (8:7).

- ▶ The law of Moses represents the old covenant (See *Exo. 19:5*).
- ▶ Even writers in the Old Testament knew a new covenant would come (*8:8-12*).
    - ▷ See *Jer. 31:31-34*.
    - ▷ God made the old covenant with His people, Israel and Judah.
    - ▷ The old covenant included spiritual promises for all people.
    - ▷ In the new covenant, God keeps the promise to bring salvation to all people.

Read *Hebrews 8:3-9*. Write down the ways the New Covenant shows God's plan for salvation.

• The New Covenant replaces the old covenant (8:13).
- ▶ God kept His promise to Abraham. Through Christ, all people have salvation.
- ▶ Christ takes the place of the law of Moses (See *Rom. 4:16-17; Gal. 3:7-9, 14; Eph. 2:12*).

Key Word
Covenant: This can mean an agreement, or it can mean a will. The author of *Hebrews* uses the word throughout *9:15-20* to show that Christ died to make the new covenant go into effect (See *9:15-18, 20; 13:20; Mat. 26:28; Gal. 3:17*).

C. Christ Serves in a Better Tabernacle (*9:1-28*)
- Moses' tabernacle was earthly (*9:1-10*).
  - ▶ A veil separated two parts of the tabernacle (*9:2-5*).
    - ▷ The first part held the lampstand (see *Exo. 25:31-40*) and a table for showbread (see *Lev. 24:5-8*) and the altar of incense (see *Exo. 30:1-6*).
    - ▷ The second part, the Most Holy part, held the Ark of the Covenant. In the Ark there were the Ten Commandments (see *Exo. 25:10-16*), a pot of manna, and Aaron's rod. The rod was a sign of authority of the priesthood.
    - ▷ On top of the ark was the mercy seat. God shows His presence there.
  - ▶ The priests led the people in worship (*9:6-10*).
    - ▷ Only the high priest went into the Most Holy place. He only went one time a year. This was the Day of Atonement (See *Lev. 16*).
    - ▷ The earthly tabernacle illustrates spiritual truth. The old system of sacrifice did not bring salvation.
- Christ's tabernacle is heavenly (*9:11-28*).
  - ▶ Christ's tabernacle is a different quality than Moses' tabernacle (9:11-15).
    - ▷ *"the eternal Spirit"* — All three Persons in the Trinity are included in cleansing (*9:14*).

    "He is the Mediator of the new covenant, by means of death, for the redemption of the transgressions under the first covenant, that those who are called may receive the promise of eternal inheritance" (*9:15*).

  - ▶ Christ is the sacrifice in the true tabernacle (*9:16-28*).
    - ▷ Christ is now the one who goes between humans and God.
    - ▷ A legal will goes into effect upon death. The death of animals put the old covenant into effect. Christ's death put the new covenant into effect.
    - ▷ Christ gave Himself as the final sacrifice.

    "He has appeared to put away sin by the sacrifice of Himself. And as it is appointed for men to die once, but after this the judgment, so Christ was offered once to bear the sins of many. To those who eagerly wait for Him He will appear a second time, apart from sin, for salvation" (*9:26b-28*).

D. Christ Is a Better Sacrifice (*10:1-18*)
- Christ's sacrifice was part of God's plan for salvation (*10:1-18*).
  - ▶ The blood of animals cannot take away sin (*10:1-4*).
    - ▷ *"things to come"* — The law instructed the people to sacrifice. This was a picture of Christ's final sacrifice.
    - ▷ The law could not bring salvation.

    "For the law, having a shadow of the good things to come, and not the very image of the things, can never with these same sac-

NOTES

rifices, which they offer continually year by year, make those who approach perfect" (10:1).

- ▶ Christ showed His obedience (*10:5-10*).
  - ▷ *"it is written of me"* — The writer quotes *Psa. 40:6-8*.
  - ▷ Even in the Old Testament, sacrifices alone did not please God.
  - ▷ God used the first system of sacrifice to point to Christ's obedience.

"He takes away the first that He may establish the second. By that we will have been sanctified through the offering of the body of Jesus Christ once for all" (10:9b-10).

- ▶ In the final sacrifice, Christ finished the work of saving humans from sin (*10:11-18*).
  - ▷ *"right hand of God"* — Christ now sits in the place of highest honor (*10:12*).
  - ▷ *"perfected forever ... being sanctified"* — God declared humans who believe "not guilty" because of Christ's final sacrifice. Now the Holy Spirit works in us to make us more like Christ (*10:14*).
- • Christ made the final sacrifice. Now humans who believe may enter the true sanctuary (*10:19-25*).
  - ▶ Jesus took away the curtain that separated humans from God (*10:20*).
  - ▶ Christ's work as High Priest is complete.
  - ▶ *"Our hearts sprinkled ... our bodies washed"* — The high priest cleaned himself before going into the Most Holy place. Christ cleans us so we can go to God.

"Let us hold fast the confession of our hope without wavering, for He who promised is faithful. And let us consider one another in order to stir up love and good works, not forsaking the assembling of ourselves together, as is the manner of some, but exhorting one another, and so much the more as you see the Day approaching" (10:23-25).

- ▶ Because Jesus takes us to God, believers can help each other in these ways:
  - ▷ Draw near to God.
  - ▷ Hold on to hope.
  - ▷ Stir up love and good works.
  - ▷ Meet together.
  - ▷ Encourage each other.
- • Word of advice: Do not return to sin (*10:26-39*).
  - ▶ *"Sin willfully"* — choosing to reject God (*10:26; see Num. 15:30-31*). This passage talks about an attitude of sinfulness, not individual sins. God is faithful to forgive sin (See *1 Joh. 1:8-9*).
  - ▶ The Christian who shows this attitude insults the Holy Spirit. God will deal with this person. This might happen in this life or at a future time of judgment (*10:29-30; see Deu. 32:35-36*).
  - ▶ *"Recall the former days"* — Readers suffered because of their faith, but they stood strong.

- ▶ *"Do not cast away your confidence"* — Do not let go of being sure of Christ (*10:35*). Some readers thought about going back to Jewish ways.
- ▶ *10:37-38* quotes from *Hab. 2:3-4*.
  - ▷ Christ will return. God will finish His plan for salvation.
  - ▷ The writer believes the readers will keep going by faith (*10:39*).

4. Faith is a Superior Principle (*11:1–13:25*)

A. <u>Examples of Faith</u> (*11:1-40*)
- Faith sees the things we hope for as real (*11:1*).

"Now faith is the substance of things hoped for, the evidence of things not seen" (*11:1*).

- The Old Testament is full of people who had true faith.
  - ▶ Abel: God accepted Abel's sacrifice because of his faith (*11:4*; see *Gen. 4:3-4*).
  - ▶ Enoch: God took him to heaven without dying (*11:5-6*; see *Gen. 5:21-14*).
  - ▶ Noah: God told Noah to build an ark, and Noah obeyed in faith (*11:7*; see *Gen. 6:13-22*).
  - ▶ Abraham: God led Abraham to a new land, and Abraham followed in faith (*11:8-10*; see *Gen. 12:1-4*).
  - ▶ Sarah: God promised Sarah would have a child who came by faith, not by human action (*11:11-12*; see *Gen. 17:19*).

"These all died in faith, not having received the promises, but having seen them afar off were assured of them, embraced them and confessed that they were strangers and pilgrims on the earth" (*11:13*).

  - ▷ These people died before Christ was born. They did not see the end of God's plan for salvation. They believed in faith that it was true (*11:13-16*).
- The writer continues with examples of faith.
  - ▶ Abraham: God tested Abraham when he told him to sacrifice his son. Abraham had faith in God's plan (*11:17-19*; see *Gen. 22*).
  - ▶ Isaac, Jacob and Joseph: They all believed God would keep His promise in the future (*11:20-22*; see *Gen. 28:26-40; 48:1-20; 50:24-25*).
  - ▶ Moses: God showed His plan for His people in the life of Moses. Moses responded with faith (*11:23-29*; see *Exo. 2:1-3, 11-15; 10:28; 12:21; 14:22-29*).
  - ▶ Joshua and Jericho: God promised His people a new land. Joshua led the people in by faith (*11:30*; see *Jos. 6:20*).
  - ▶ Rahab: She was not an Israelite, but God saved her because of her faith (*11:31*; see *Jos. 6:23*).
  - ▶ Many more were people of faith: Gideon (see *Jud. 6:11*), Barak (*Jud. 4:6-24*), Samson (*Jud. 13:24*), Jephthah (*Jud. 11:1-29*), David (*1 Sam. 16:17*), Samuel (*1 Sam. 7:9-14*).

NOTES

Key Word
Faith: The writer of *Hebrews* stresses the promise of faith. The examples of faith show both what people could not see and what God planned. People who have the promise take action by faith.[55]

> ▶ *"Some faced jeers and flogging..."* — (*11:35-38*) Not everyone who has faith will be delivered from suffering and pain in this world, but they will be rewarded in the world to come.

What is your response to the fact that suffering and pain is sometimes God's way of working in our life?

    B. <u>Enduring Faith</u> (*12:1-13*)
- Jesus is the supreme example of faith (*12:1-3*).

"Therefore we also, since we are surrounded by so great a cloud of witnesses, let us lay aside every weight, and the sin which so easily ensnares us, and let us run with endurance the race that is set before us, looking unto Jesus, the author and finisher of our faith, who for the joy that was set before Him endured the cross, despising the shame, and has sat down at the right hand of the throne of God" (*12:1-2*).

> ▶ *"Therefore"* — This word connects the previous teaching with action in the spiritual life (*12:1*).
> ▶ *"Cloud of witnesses"* — This is athletic imagery. Athletes are surrounded as they run the race.
>> ▷ The witnesses are the people mentioned in *chapter 11*. They ran the race of faith in their lives.
>> ▷ The witnesses show us the truth of faith. Their example inspires us.[56]
> ▶ *"Lay aside every weight"* — Runners take off anything that slows them down, even certain clothing (*12:1*; see *Col. 3:8*).
> ▶ *"The race that is set before us"* — We are not running without a goal. We are not running for exercise. We are running toward the finish line (*12:1*; see *Rom. 12:12*).
> ▶ *"Looking unto Jesus"* — If we look around during the race, we will slow down. Focus on Christ (*12:2*).
> ▶ *"The author and finisher"* — Our faith comes from Christ (see *2:10*) and Christ has done everything we need for salvation (*12:2*).
> ▶ *"The joy that was set before Him..."* — Christ ran toward the finish line. This is the reason to keep running (*12:2b-3*; see *Luk. 24:26*).
>> ▷ Christ endured the cross. He paid no attention to the disgrace of the cross. He focused on the goal of salvation.

NOTES

▷ Christ gives us an example of running toward the goal with joy. This might mean suffering.
▶ When He finished the race, Christ sat at *"God's right hand"*, a place of honor (*12:2;* see *Phi. 2:8-11*).
▶ *"Consider how…"* In three verses (*12:1-3*), the writer points to Christ's example three times.

How do the examples of other people's faith help you in your faith?

How does Jesus' example of faith help you?

- Faith lasts in hard times (*12:4-13*).
  ▶ God disciplines His children out of love (4:5-8; see Pro. 3:11-12).
  ▶ *"Endure hardship as discipline"* — Even suffering helps train us to follow Christ and run the race (*4:9-11*).
    ▷ Earthly fathers train their children for their own good. Our heavenly Father disciplines us to make us holy.
    ▷ *"fruit of righteousness"* – The benefit of hardship comes later.
  ▶ See *Isa. 35:5*. Believers build up their strength to run the race (*12:12-13*).
- Word of advice: Do not refuse God (*12:14-29*).
  ▶ Pursue holy living by avoiding dangers (*12:14-17*).

  "Pursue peace with all people, and holiness, without which no one will see the Lord: looking carefully lest anyone fall short of the grace of God" (*12:14-15a*).

  ▷ Do not refuse God's offer of salvation (*12:15*).
  ▷ Do not allow bitterness to grow among believers (*12:15*).
  ▷ Do not be sexually immoral (*12:16*).[57]
  ▷ Do not be profane. Esau gave up his inheritance. He put more value on food than on God's promise (*12:16-17*).
  ▶ Two mountains: Mount Sinai and Mount Zion (*12:18-29*).
    ▷ *"mountain"* — Moses received God's law on Mount Sinai. God showed His holiness. The people shook with fear. This is the old covenant (*12:18-21*; see *Deu. 4:11; 5:11; Exo. 20:18-26*).
    ▷ Believers receive God's grace in the heavenly Mount Zion. This is the new covenant (*12:22-24*; see *Exo. 24:8; Gen. 4:10*).

NOTES
- ▶ God revealed more by grace than by law (*12:25-29*).
  - ▷ Greater knowledge brings greater danger (See *2:2-3*).
  - ▷ *"consuming fire"* — God's judgment on those who refuse Him (*12:29;* see *Deu. 4:24*).

C. <u>Directions for Christian Life in Daily Practice</u> (*13:1-17*)
- Rules for Christian living (*13:1-17*).
  - ▶ Love is the first rule (*13:1*).
  - ▶ Practice hospitality. You may be helping someone God sent (*13:2;* see *Gen. 18-19; Jud. 6, Rom. 12:10*).
  - ▶ Remember those who suffer. *"Remember the prisoners"* — believers persecuted for faith (*3:3*).[58]
  - ▶ Do not defile the body (*13:4;* see *Pro. 5:18-19; 1 Cor. 6:9*).
  - ▶ Do not covet (*13:5-6;* see *Deu. 31:6, 8*).
  - ▶ Respect leaders (*13:7, 17-18*).
    - ▷ Church leaders, elders should be examples of how to live the life of faith that they are teaching about.
    - ▷ Good elders are like faithful shepherds watching the flock and who deeply care for the sheep. They will give an account to God one day for those within their flock.
  - ▶ Hang on to right teaching (*13:8-9*).
  - ▶ Worship spiritually (*13:10-16*).
- The writer asks for prayer (*13:18-19*).
- Personal remarks and benedictions (*13:20-25*).

Suggestions for Preaching From *Hebrews*

- Show the difference between the Old Testament system of sacrifice and Christ's sacrifice of Himself for us.

- Study the connection between faith and endurance in times of trials.

- Find the ways the author encourages spiritual maturity, rather than immaturity.

CHAPTER TWELVE
JAMES

The New Testament mentions five men named James: James the brother of John, both disciples (Mat. 4:21); James the son of Alphaeus, another disciple (Mat. 10:3); the father of Judas (Luk. 6:16); and James, the half-brother of Jesus (Mat. 13:55). Jesus' brother became the leader of the church in Jerusalem (Act. 15:3; Gal. 2:9). He is the most likely author of the book of *James*.

James did not send this letter to one church. Readers were Christians who lived outside of Palestine. *James* often talks about those who are poor and suffering. It is possible readers suffered because of their faith. James wrote sometime between AD 44 and 62.[59]

Many books in the New Testament teach doctrines of the Christian faith. *James* has a practical purpose. The author seems to say, "If you believe in Jesus, your actions will show it." He often uses figures of speech to express an idea. He gives many examples. The book is a series of short sections, rather than long theological ideas. Some commentators say that the book of *James* is the "Proverbs" of the New Testament.

What to watch for:

Key words: faith and works, brothers, trials.

Tip: Open your Bible to *James* so you can follow the readings.

1. Introduction (*1:2-18*)

   A. <u>Respond to Trials from the Outside</u> (*1:2-11*)
   - Look at trials with joy (*1:2-4*).
     ▶ *"Testing of your faith"* — Testing proves what is true. Testing showed if a coin was real (*1:2;* see *1 Pet. 1:7*). Testing of coins and select material was often done by fire.
     ▶ *"Patience"* — God is at work in our trials helping us stand up under pressure. God's work brings joy (*2:3-4*).
   - Meet trials with faith (*1:5-8*).
     ▶ Ask God for wisdom. He gives generously (*1:5;* see *Psa. 111:10; Pro. 9:10*).
     ▶ Ask in faith. "Doubt" is a divided mind. This does not mean being unsure in the moment. It means having two loyalties in your life (*5:6-7*).
   - Riches are not the answer to life's troubles (*1:9-11*).
     ▶ *"Lowly"* — be glad to see God at work in your life (*1:9*).
     ▶ *"Rich"* — humility means depending on God, not your riches (*1:10*).
     ▶ Life is short. Depend on God (*1:11;* see "The Parable of the Rich Fool" — *Luk.12:13-21*).

NOTES

Key Word

Trials: When we face troubles, we see if our faith is true. Trials make our faith more pure. Christ's example shows us how to respond to suffering.

    B. <u>Respond to Temptations from the Inside</u> (*1:12–18*)
- Temptation comes from within us (*1:12-15*).
  - ▶ *"Crown of life"* — The Bible uses several pictures of the believer's reward at judgment (*1:12;* see *2 Cor. 5:10; 1 Cor. 3:8-13; 9:25; Rev. 2:10; 3:5; 22:12*).
  - ▶ Temptations do not come from God. God does not try to make people sin (*1:13*).

  "Let no one say when he is tempted, "I am tempted by God;" for God cannot be tempted by evil, nor does He Himself tempt anyone. But each one is tempted when he is drawn away by his own desires and enticed" (*1:13-14*).

  - ▶ Temptations come from our desires (*1:14-15*).
    - ▷ Trials become temptations when desire makes us want something.
    - ▷ Desire becomes sin, and sin becomes action that leads to death.
    - ▷ Temptation has three stages: desire, sin and death (See *Gen. 3:6-22* and *2 Sam. 11:2-17*).
- God gives us good and perfect gifts (*1:16-18*).
  - ▶ God the Creator is the One who gives us life and salvation.

  "Every good gift and every perfect gift is from above, and comes down from the Father of lights, with whom there is no variation or shadow of turning" (*1:17*).

  - ▶ *"Good and perfect gift"* — literally this means, "every good act of giving." Humans cannot give the gifts God gives (1:17).[60]
  - ▶ Our experiences on earth may shift and change. God, who gives to us, does not change (*1:18*).

2. Main Themes: Being Swift to Hear, Slow to Speak, Slow to Wrath (*1:19-20*)

"So then, my beloved brethren, let every man be swift to hear, slow to speak, slow to wrath; for the wrath of man does not produce the righteousness of God" (*1:19-20*).

- These ideas are the main idea of the rest of the book of James.
- When we do not live these ideas, we do not bring glory to God.

3. Be Quick to Hear (*1:21–2:26*)

    A. <u>Good Works Result from Hearing the Word of God</u> (*1:21-27*)

- Be people who hear God's Word (*1:21*).
  - ▶ *"Receive the implanted word"* — God plants His Word in us. We must be soil where it can take root.[61]
- Be people who take action on what they hear (*1:22-25*).
  - ▶ To hear the Word and not obey it means we are deceived (*1:22*; see *Mat. 7:21-28*).
  - ▶ *"Perfect law of liberty"* — the law of love (*1:25*; see *Mat. 26:36-40; Eph. 3:17-19*).
- True religion shows in actions (*1:26-27*).

"If anyone among you thinks he is religious, and does not bridle his tongue but deceives his own heart, this one's religion is useless. Pure and undefiled religion before God and the Father is this: to visit orphans and widows in their trouble, and to keep oneself unspotted from the world" (*1:26-27*).

- ▶ *"Religious"* — outward acts of religion.[62] (See *Act. 26:5; Col. 2:18*).
- ▶ True religion is not based on ceremonies. It is doing what God wants us to do in the world without taking on values of the world.

B. <u>Do Not Show Personal Favorites</u> (*2:1-13*)
- Respect all persons (*2:1-7*).
  - ▶ *"Faith of our Lord Jesus Christ"* — Christ died for the world. Treat every person as someone God loves (*2:1*).
  - ▶ How would you treat a rich person? How would you treat a poor person? Give both the same respect without judging (*2:2-4*).
  - ▶ God values the poor. He makes them rich in faith (*2:5*).
  - ▶ Being rich might make people too proud. The poor deserve honor (*2:6-7*).

Key Word
Brothers: James uses this word 15 times. He writes to correct actions, but he writes with brotherly love.

- Fulfill the royal law (*2:8-13*).
  - ▶ This is the law of love. Love is the highest principle for how we obey God (*2:8*; see *Lev. 19:18; Mat. 22:39*).
  - ▶ Showing favorites is the opposite of the law of love (*2:9*).
  - ▶ *"Guilty of all"* — We cannot pick and choose the ways we will please God. We must decide to follow the law of love even when we do not want to.
  - ▶ If we fail in one part, we fail in all parts of the law (*2:10-11*).
  - ▶ *"Law of liberty"* — the royal law of love gives freedom to obey (*2:12*).
  - ▶ *"Judgment"* — This is not judgment about salvation. James writes to people who believe. Rather this judgment gives rewards to believers (*2:12-13*; see *1 Cor. 3:12-15; 2 Cor. 5:10; Rev 22:12*).

C. <u>Faith and Works Go Together</u> (*2:14-26*)
- Faith without works is dead (*2:14-20*).

NOTES

NOTES

"What does it profit, my brethren, if someone says he has faith but does not have works? Can faith save him?" (2:14).

- ▶ James is not saying that faith does not save. Rather, faith that is only in the mind is not true faith. We only truly believe what we live.
- ▶ James uses a practical example.
- ▶ *"Faith by itself ... is dead"* — This faith is in the mind only. It has not changed the heart. It was never alive (*2:17*).

Use your own words to explain what James says about faith and works.

"But someone will say, 'You have faith, and I have works.' Show me your faith without works, and I will show you my faith by my works" (2:18).

- ▶ There are not "faith Christians" and "work Christians."
- ▶ True faith in Jesus will eventually show itself in actions toward others.
- ▶ Even demons know there is one true God. Knowing in your mind is not faith (*2:19*).
- ▶ Faith and works are not separate from each other. It is foolish to try to have one and not the other (*2:20*).
- Abraham and Rahab are examples of faith at work (*2:21-26*).
    - ▶ Abraham obeyed God when he put his son on the altar. He did not earn salvation this way. Rather, he showed his faith (*2:21-24*).
        - ▷ Faith leads to action. Actions make faith complete.
        - ▷ God declared Abraham "not guilty" because of his faith (*2:23*; see *Gen. 15:6; Rom. 3:28; Rom. 4:3; Gal. 2:15-16*).
    - ▶ Rahab helped the spies from Israel because she believed in God (*2:25*; see *Jos. 2; Heb. 11:31*).

Key words
Faith and Works: The apostle Paul uses "faith" and "works" in his letters. When Paul says "works," he means human efforts to keep the Jewish legal law. He says this is impossible to do. God calls us "not guilty" of breaking the law because Christ kept the law. God saves us by faith. In James, "works" means the practical actions of Christians. These "works" show true faith. Because we have faith, we show it in our actions.

4. Be Slow to Speak (*3:1-18*)

A. <u>Control the Tongue</u> (*3:1-12*)
- Teachers have special responsibility (*3:1-5a*).

"My brethren, let not many of you become teachers, knowing that we shall receive a stricter judgment" (3:1).

NOTES

- ▶ Teachers use the tongue to teach about God's truth. But it is easy to misuse the tongue. What we teach reflects our lives.
- ▶ Everyone sins (2:2).
- ▶ A small action, even a word, can have a big result.
  - ▷ *"bridle the whole body"* — (2:2-3). A small bit in the horse's mouth controls the whole animal. Holding back wrong words keeps the whole body from doing wrong.
  - ▷ *"rudder"* — a small piece turns the whole ship (2:4a).
- The tongue is powerful (3:5b-12).

"See how great a forest a little fire kindles! And the tongue is a fire, a world of iniquity" (3:5b-6).

- ▶ *"Defiles the whole body"* — Using the tongue to speak in the wrong way is the beginning of many sins (3:6; see *Pro. 16:27; Mat. 12:36*).
- ▶ *"Course of nature"* — The tongue affects the whole life (3:6).
- ▶ *"Set on fire by hell"* — This contrasts with the purifying fire of the Holy Spirit (3:6; see *Act. 2:2-4; Isa. 6:5*).

Why do you think James writes so much about what believers say?

- ▶ Humans tame wild animals, but they cannot tame their own tongues (2:7-8).
  - ▷ *"unruly evil, full of deadly poison"* — only God can tame the tongue (See *Eph. 4:29; 5:4*).
- ▶ *"Similitude of God"* — God created humans in His image (3:9; see Gen. *1:26*). All people reflect God's image. To curse another person dishonors God.

"Does a spring send forth fresh water and bitter from the same opening? Can a fig tree, my brethren, bear olives, or a grapevine bear figs? Thus no spring yields both salt water and fresh" (3:11-12).

  - ▷ We use the same tongue to bless the Lord and curse others.
  - ▷ If the tongue is out of control, we are not really blessing God.
  - ▷ Tips for Taming the Tongue:
    - ◆ Remember that words can harm or heal (*Pro. 12:18*).
    - ◆ Speak the truth in love (*Eph. 4:15, 25*).
    - ◆ Speak with grace and use words that build up, not words that attack (*Eph. 4:29*).

- Listen before we speak (*Pro. 18:13*).
- Take time to know the real meaning behind a person's words (*Pro. 20:5*).
- Pray for God to help us with our words (*Psa. 141:3*).
- Keep our disagreements with others confidential (*Pro. 16:28; 25:9*).
- Do not be involved with quarrels. It is possible to disagree in an agreeable way (*Pro. 17:14; 20:3*).
- If someone criticizes you or attacks you, do not respond in the same way (*Rom. 12:17, 21; 1 Pet. 2:23*).

B. <u>Act Wisely Before Speaking</u> (*3:13-18*)
- Good conduct shows wisdom (*3:13-16*).
  - *"Wise and understanding ... meekness of wisdom"* — Knowledge alone is not enough. Wisdom makes a difference in our lives (*3:13; see Deu. 1:13; Isa. 5:21*).
    - Wisdom uses knowledge to please God.
    - *"meekness of wisdom"* — compared to pride of knowledge.
  - Prideful wisdom is human wisdom. It brings confusion.
- True wisdom comes from God (*3:17-18*).

"But the wisdom that is from above is first pure, then peaceable, gentle, willing to yield, full of mercy, without partiality and without hypocrisy" (*3:17*).

  - Characteristics of wisdom (*3:17*).
  - *"Fruit of righteousness"* — results from wisdom that God gives (*3:18*).

5. Be Slow to Wrath (*4:1–5:12*)

A. <u>Solve Conflict through Humility</u> (*4:1-10*)
- Conflicts come from selfish desires (*4:1-5*).
  - *"Wars and fights"* — come from our sinful desires (*4:1*).
  - James is writing to believers. Christians fall into these sins (*4:2*).
  - *"Ask amiss"* — Pray for God's will, not your own desires (*4:2-3*).
  - When we want what the world offers, we move away from God (*4:4-5; see 1 Joh. 2:15; Gal. 1:4; Gen. 6:5*).
- Living in God's grace means living with humility (*4:6-10*).

"God resists the proud, but gives grace to the humble" (*4:6*).

  - Submit to God's wisdom and receive the grace you need (See *Pro. 3:34*).
  - Commands call for action.
    - Submit to God (*4:7*).
    - Resist the devil (*4:7; see Eph. 6:10-20*).
    - Draw near to God (*4:8*).
    - Cleanse your hands (*4:8; see Exo. 30:17-21; Psa. 24:4*).

▷ Purify your hearts (*4:8;* see *1 Pet. 1:22*).
▷ Lament, mourn, weep. Turn laughter to mourning, joy to gloom (4:9). These are words of repentance. Do not celebrate sin.
▷ Humble yourselves (4:10). (See Mat. 23:12; 1 Pet. 5:6).

How do these commands in *4:7-10* show a humble spirit?

B. <u>Withhold Judgment</u> (*4:11-12*)
- Do not judge each other (*4:11;* see *Mat. 7:1*).
- When we judge each other, we do not practice the law of love.
- God is the Judge (*4:12;* see *Rom. 14:4*).

C. <u>Rely on God and Don't Be Proud</u> (*4:13-17*)
- It is not wrong to make a plan. It is wrong to leave God out of the plan (*4:13-15;* see *Pro. 17:1*).
  ▶ We don't know the future, but God does.
  ▶ We cannot plan our lives based on human knowledge alone. Depend on God.
   ▷ Because our lives are so short, and like a vapor, we cannot brag about what we will do for God tomorrow.
   ▷ But if you know something you are supposed to do today and put it off then to you it is the sin of presumption (*4:13-17*).
- Sinful attitudes keep us from depending on God (*4:16-17;* see *1 Cor. 5:6*).

D. <u>When Someone Treats You Unjustly, Be Patient</u> (*5:1-12*)
- If you are rich, be careful not to be proud (*5:1-6*).
  ▶ James wrote to rich people who misused their money to work against the poor.
  ▶ This attitude toward money stores up judgment (*5:1*).
   ▷ James writes in a style of Old Testament prophets who announced judgment against the rich (See *Isa. 3:14-15; 10:2*).
   ▷ God will judge people who hold down the poor (See *Eze. 18:12-13*).
  ▶ Earthly riches do not have spiritual value (*5:2*).
   ▷ "garments," "gold and silver" — signs of wealth.
  ▶ The rich saved up large amounts of money (*5:3*). They did not pay their workers (*5:4*). They lived for pleasure (*5:5b*).
  ▶ It is not wrong to enjoy what God gives. It is wrong to get rich by causing others to suffer.
- If you suffer, wait for God (*5:7-11*).
  ▶ Believers suffered at the hands of the rich. The response is to look forward to the Lord's coming.
  ▶ Watch your attitude. Be patient. Do not grumble.

NOTES

NOTES

"My brethren, take the prophets, who spoke in the name of the Lord, as an example of suffering and patience. Indeed we count them blessed who endure. You have heard of the perseverance of Job and seen the end intended by the Lord—that the Lord is very compassionate and merciful" (5:10-11).

- ▶ The prophets waited for God to act. Many of them suffered while they waited. See *Mat. 5:12* and the stories of Elijah and Jeremiah.
- ▶ The Lord honored Job's perseverance with blessings.
- Keep your word (*5:12*).
    - ▶ James does not mean a believer can never take a solemn oath.
    - ▶ He speaks against using God's name in a casual way as proof you are speaking the truth.
    - ▶ If you say yes, then mean yes. The Lord highly values integrity.

6. Concluding Prayer (*5:13-20*)

A. <u>Prayer and Praise Are Powerful</u> (*5:13-18*)
- The suffering may pray, even as others are happy (*5:13*).
    - ▶ Prayer can give us grace to endure suffering (See *4:6* and *2 Cor. 12:7-10*).
- The sick may pray (*5:14-16*).
    - ▶ "*Elders*" — people in authority in the church. The New Testament also calls these people "bishops." (See *1 Tim. 3:1; 5:17; Tit 1:5-9*).
    - ▶ "*Anointing him with oil*" — healing power of the Holy Spirit.
    - ▶ "*Prayer of faith*" — All healing comes from God.
    - ▶ "*If he has committed sins*" — Sin does not always cause sickness. But the sick person who has sinned should confess. Sickness is not always a result of a person's sin, but self examination and action is required.
- Follow Elijah's example and pray sincerely (*5:17-18*).

B. <u>Bring Back Those Who Go Astray</u> (*5:19-20*)
- "*Wanders from the truth*" — believers who have lost their way (*5:19*).
- Others should help wanderers find their way back.
    - ▶ "*Cover a multitude of sins*" — Old Testament image for forgiveness (See *Psa. 32:1*).
    - ▶ The goal is to restore the person to the church and fellowship in the local Body of Christ.

Suggestions for Preaching From *James*

- Explore the theme of faith in times of trials.

- Teach on the figurative literal language and what James teaches with each image.

- Focus on the dangers and opportunities of the tongue.

Figures of Speech in the Book of *James*: Read each verse in its context. What does the figure of speech mean?

NOTES

1:6 ......Wave of the sea

1:9 ......Flower of the field

1:17 ....Shadow

1:23 ....Looking in a mirror

3:2-3 ...Bridle, bits

3:4 ......Rudder

3:6 ......Fire

3:18 ....Deadly poison

3:12 ....Fresh water, salt water

3:18 ....Harvest

4:13 ....Vapor

4:5 ......Fattened hearts, slaughter

CHAPTER THIRTEEN
1 PETER

Peter, one of the first twelve disciples of Jesus, wrote the books of *1* and *2 Peter*. His readers were scattered throughout Asia Minor (modern day Turkey). Most likely Peter was in Rome when he wrote. He says he is "in Babylon" (*5:13*). The New Testament often uses "Babylon" as a symbol for Rome, the center of the Roman Empire (*Rev. 14:8; 16:19; 17:5; 18:2*). Peter's readers also would know Babylon was a place of exile, as it was in the Old Testament. Tradition tells us that Peter died in Rome during a period of persecution. This happened while Nero was emperor, AD 54–68. Most likely, Peter wrote around AD 62–64.

Peter wrote his first letter to encourage readers who suffered because of their Christian faith. Christians became outcasts because they no longer worshiped pagan gods. Often they left one city because of persecution and looked for safety in a new place only to find more suffering. Peter wrote to remind them they were pilgrims in this world. Their final destination was heaven.

What to watch for:

Key words: holy/holiness, suffer.

Tip: Open your Bible to *1 Peter* so you can follow the readings.

1. Comfort in Suffering (*1:1-25*)

    A. Greetings (*1:1-2*)
- *"Elect according to the foreknowledge of God"* — (See *Eph. 1:4; Rom. 8:29*). Exiled and dispersed people need to remember the secure position and future they have as the elect in Christ. No one can take this away. We may wander from our physical home due to suffering, but our eternal home will always be secure.

- *"Sanctification"* — The Holy Spirit influences believers to move away from sin and into holiness (See *2 The. 2:13*).

    B. God Gives Grace in This Life and the Future (*1:3-12*)

"Blessed be the God and Father of our Lord Jesus Christ, who according to His abundant mercy has begotten us again to a living hope through the resurrection of Jesus Christ from the dead" (*1:3*).

- Christians have a future hope (*1:3-5*). Peter talks about suffering often (See *1:6; 2:12; 18-25; 3:13-18; 4:1, 4, 12-19; 5:1, 7-10*). Peter always responds to suffering with hope. *"Living hope"* indicates the undying and permanent nature of this hope.

NOTES

- ▶ Christian hope is not wishful thinking. It is firm confidence.
- ▶ Our confidence is based on Jesus because God raised Him from the dead.
- Hope in the future gives purpose and perspective to trials in the present (*1:6-9*).
  - ▶ We live in joy, even in suffering (*1:6, 8*).
  - ▶ Trials make faith deeper and show it is true, just as heat shows that gold is pure (*1:7*).
  - ▶ We rejoice because we are receiving our salvation now. Each day takes us closer to the final day (*1:9*). Believers already enjoy essential elements of their salvation, such as peace and fellowship with God and other Christians, but full possession awaits Christ's return.
- Our living hope springs from what God said in the past (*1:10-12*).
  - ▶ The Old Testament prophets knew that one day salvation would come (*1:10*).
  - ▶ The Holy Spirit spoke through the prophets (*1:11-12*).

C. Holiness Follows New Birth (*1:13-25*)
   - Peter begins a series of commands for holy living that continue for the rest of the letter. God is holy and wants to make us holy (*1:13-16*).

Key Word

Holy/Holiness: Peter uses this word seven times in his two letters in a way that talks about holy living (*1:5, 15-16; 2:9; 3:5*). We cannot be holy by ourselves. The Holy Spirit transforms us and gives us the ability to resist sin. Holy living shows that Christians are God's people while we wait for Christ to return.

- Our salvation comes at a price. Christ paid the price (*1:17-21*).
  - ▶ The fear of God is the reason for holy living (*1:17*).
  - ▶ Peter again points to our future hope (*1:21*).
- Obeying God's truth shows in our relationships (*1:22-25*).
  - ▶ Sincere love is the mark of believers (*1:21-22*; see *Rom. 12:9; Joh. 13:24-25; 1 The. 4:9-10*).
  - ▶ *"Word of God"* — brings people to God in new birth (*1:23-34*).
    - ▷ The prophets knew God's Word. Peter preached God's Word.
    - ▷ God's Word calls people to repent of sin.
    - ▷ God's Word lasts forever

2. Holiness Shows in Practical Living (*2:1–3:22*)

A. Holiness Begins in Our Experience of the Lord (*2:1-3*)
   - *"Therefore"* — Because of what God has done, we are different (*2:1*). The placement of these vices in this verse implies that they can very much hinder the Christian's appetite for God's Word.
     - ▶ Peter warns his readers to avoid malice, deceit, hypocrisy, envy and slander.
     - ▶ Listing these evil actions in this verse suggests they can much hinder the Christian's hunger for God's Word.
   - *"Desire the pure milk"* — Be hungry for God's Word the way a baby is hungry for milk (*2:2-3*).

NOTES

- ▶ *"Milk"* is not the same as in *1 Cor. 3:2; Heb. 5:12-14.* In those passages, drinking milk is a picture of immaturity.
- ▶ Peter's point is to be hungry for God's Word.

B. <u>Live as Holy People</u> (*2:4-10*)
- God is building a spiritual house in His people (*2:4-5*).
  - ▶ *"Living stone"* — In contrast to dead stone idols.[64]
  - ▶ *"Holy priesthood"* — In the Old Testament, only some people were priests. In the New Testament, all believers are priests (*2:5;* see *Heb. 7:26; Heb. 10:10*).
- Jesus is the foundation of the spiritual house (*2:6-8*).
  - ▶ Peter quotes the Old Testament (See *Isa. 18:16; Psa. 118:22; Isa. 8:14*).
  - ▶ *"Stumble"* — Unbelief can only lead to destruction (*2:8*).[65]
  - ▶ Christians belong to God (*2:9-10*).

"But you are a chosen generation, a royal priesthood, a holy nation, His own special people, that you may proclaim the praises of Him who called you out of darkness into His marvelous light" (*2:9*).

- ▶ *"Chosen people"* — See *Eph. 1:4; Isa. 43:10, 20; Isa. 44:1-2.* This term now includes both Jewish and Gentile believers.
- ▶ *"Royal priesthood"* — See *Exo. 19:6; Rev 1:6.*
- ▶ *"Holy nation"* — Believers are set apart for God to use.
- ▶ *"His own special people"* — See *Exo. 19:5; Rom. 9:25-26.*

C. <u>Respond to Persecution with Good Lives</u> (*2:11-3:13*)
- Bring glory to God with good deeds (*2:11-12*).
- Bring glory to God with good citizenship (*2:13-17*).
  - ▶ Respect the authority of government (*2:13-14*).
  - ▶ The best defense against accusations is good conduct (*2:15-16*).
  - ▶ Respect other citizens out of respect for God (*2:17*).
- Even slaves can submit of their own free will (*2:18-25*).
  - ▶ About one-third of the people in the Roman Empire were slaves.[66]
    - ▷ Serve with respect (*2:18*).
    - ▷ Serve willingly even in unfair situations (*2:19-21*).
  - ▶ Jesus submitted to God because He trusted God. He is our example in suffering (*2:21-25*).
- Wives and husbands must both show respect (*3:1-7*).
  - ▶ Submission does not mean wives hold a lower status. By their respect in the home, wives may help husbands come to faith (*3:1-6;* see *Eph. 5:22*).
  - ▶ Husbands treat wives with respect and equals in faith (*3:7;* see Eph. 5:25).
- Show Christian unity in relationships (*3:8-22*).

"Finally, all of you be of one mind, having compassion for one another; love as brothers, be tenderhearted, be courteous; not returning evil for evil or reviling for reviling, but on the contrary blessing, knowing that you were called to this, that you may inherit a blessing" (*3:8-9*).

NOTES

- ▶ Do not let the world set the standard for relationships (See *Psa. 34:12-16; 37:27; Jas. 1:26; Rom. 12:18*).
- ▶ *"Sanctify the Lord God in your hearts"* — Set aside Christ as Lord. If you do this, then speaking the reason for hope will match your actions (*3:15*).
- ▶ *"Spirits in prison"* — several possible meanings.
- ▶ Jesus went to the place where fallen angels were (See *Gen. 6:1-4; Jude 1:6*).
  - ▷ Jesus preached to humans who had died in the time of Noah.
  - ▷ Jesus preached through Noah to people in his day who did not believe.[67]
  - ▷ The disobedient spirits in prison are angels, authorities and powers mentioned in *3:22*. When Christ was raised and ascended to heaven, this declared victory.[68]

3. Suffering Has Spiritual Significance (*4:1-19*)

A. <u>Physical Suffering, Spiritual Meaning</u> (*4:1-6*)
   - *"Give an account"* — Everyone faces judgment, including those who cause suffering (*4:5*).
   - *"To those who are dead"* — those who are spiritually dead. The Gospel offers spiritual life (*4:6*).[69]

B. <u>Love One Another Despite Suffering</u> (*4:7-11*)
   - Looking for Christ's return influences believers' actions.
   - The goal is always to bring praise to God.

C. <u>Persecution Means We Participate in Christ's Suffering</u> (*4:12-19*)
   - *"Do not be surprised"* — Christians can expect to suffer (*4:12*; see *Col. 1:24*).
   - *"Blessed ... rests upon you"* — When Christians suffer for Christ, they may find a close relationship with God (*4:14*).
   - *"Faithful Creator"* — We trust God, who controls all things.

Key Word
Suffer: Peter clearly expects believers will suffer. He does not teach about how to avoid suffering. Rather, he stresses the spiritual benefits that can come from suffering (*1 Pet. 1:6-7; 5:10*). He also reminds readers that Jesus suffered (*1 Pet. 3:18*).

4. Love Guides Life Together (*5:1-11*)

A. <u>Love and Humility Lead to Service</u> (5:1-7)
   - *"Elders"* should lead with love and willingness (*5:1-2*).
   - *"Fellow elder"* — Peter identifies himself with the elders so he can better encourage them.
   - All relationships should show humility (*5:3-7*).

B. <u>God's Grace Helps Us Resist the Devil</u> (*5:8-11*)
   - The devil is active. Believers must be prepared (*5:8-9*).
   - Peter points again to the future hope of Christians (*5:10-11*).

5. Closing and Blessing (*5:12-14*)

NOTES

Look back through the book of *1 Peter*. What does Peter say about each of these topics?

Salvation:

Suffering:

God's People:

Christian Life:

Judgment:

Hope:

Suggestions for Preaching From *1 Peter*

- Identify Peter's teaching on comfort and hope for believers during persecution.

- Explore the connections between members of the community of Christ.

- Teach on how we are accountable to God because of His coming judgment.

CHAPTER FOURTEEN
2 PETER

The second letter of Peter talks about false teaching. Peter most likely wrote *2 Peter* sometime between AD 64 and 68. His purpose was to speak against the false teachers so that his readers would not accept wrong teaching as truth. Peter stressed the coming day of the Lord, when God will judge all people and bring in the new heaven and new earth. He urges readers to hang on to the truth while they wait for Christ to return.

What to watch for

Key word: Day of the Lord.

Tip: Open your Bible to *2 Peter* so you can follow the readings.

1. Greeting (*1:1-4*)

"*A faith precious as ours ...*" — Peter wants these Christians to realize that there are no second class Christians. The apostles did not have a better faith than anyone else.

2. Faith Results in Virtue (*1:5-15*)

A. <u>Christians Grow in Faithfulness</u> (*1:5-9*)
- "*Add*" — qualities that show a fruitful Christian life (*1:5;* see *Gal. 5:22-23*).

"But also for this very reason, giving all diligence, add to your faith virtue, to virtue knowledge, to knowledge self-control, to self-control perseverance, to perseverance godliness, to godliness brotherly kindness, and to brotherly kindness love" (*1:5-7*).

- "*Knowledge*" — False teachers taught that spiritual knowledge meant Christians did not have to show self-control. Peter says knowledge leads to self-control.

B. <u>We Live Out God's Calling With These Virtues</u> (*1:10-11*)
- God calls us to obedience and holiness (See *1 Pet. 1:2; Eph. 1:3-6*).
  - ▶ "*Making your calling and election sure*" — Although God's elect are sure and firm in God (*2 Tim. 2:19*), the individual Christian needs to live this out.
  - ▶ The evidence of the true calling of the elect is the Holy Spirit's work in our lives (*1 Joh. 3:10*), and the Holy Spirit's internal testimony in our hearts (*Gal. 4:6*).
- "*Never stumble*" — Peter's focus is on our confidence in God. Election is

NOTES

no excuse for immaturity. We continue to grow in faith, action and holiness.

C. <u>Remember What You Have Learned</u> (*1:12-15*)
- *"Christ showed me"* — This may refer to *Joh. 21:18-19*, or it may mean Peter received a revelation (*2:14*).
- Peter knows he will die soon and wants to leave a lasting teaching of the truth (*2:15*).

3. Christ's Divine Authority (*1:16-21*)

A. <u>Peter Was an Eyewitness to Jesus</u> (*1:16-18*)
- Peter did not make up his own teaching. He passed on the teaching he received directly from Jesus (*1:16*).
- *"We heard this voice"* — Peter was present at the Transfiguration of Jesus (See *Mat. 17:1-13*). James and John were there too.

B. <u>Scripture Proves Jesus Is Who He Said He Was</u> (*1:19-21*)
- *"Light that shines"* — The world is dark with sin. God's Word brings light to the believer. The light points to the time when Christ will return (*1:19*).[70]
- The prophets did not make up their own message. The message came from God (*2:20-21*).

Why does Peter stress Scripture comes from God?

4. False Prophets and Teachers (*2:1-22*)

A. <u>Be Careful About False Teachers</u> (*2:1-3*)
- *"Denying the Lord"* — False teachers would come in secretly and teach wrong doctrine.
- *"Destruction does not slumber"* — Though it looks like God is not judging false teachers, judgment will come.

B. <u>God Judged False Teachers in the Past</u> (*2:4-9*)
- God judged the angels who followed Satan's sin (*2:4*; see *Jude 6-10*).
- God judged the ungodly people of Noah's day (*2:5*; see *Gen. 6:5-12*).
- God judged Sodom and Gomorrah for wickedness (*2:6-8*; see *Gen. 19:1-26*).
- If God judged these people, He certainly will judge the false teachers (*2:9-10*).

C. False Teachers Show Evil, Not Truth (*2:10-16*)
  • The false teachers of Peter's time faced judgment because they followed the sinful nature (*2:10-14*).
  • The false teachers faced judgment because they rejected authority (*2:15-16*).

D. False Teachings are Useless (*2:17-22*)
  • False teaching seems full, but it is empty (*2:17-18*).
  • False teachers promise liberty, but they are slaves to sin (*2:19-20*).
  • *"Better ... not to have known"* — If knowledge does not lead to obedience, it is no good (*2:21-22*; see *Mat. 26:24*).

How are false teachers dangerous to Christians?

5. Christ Will Return (*3:1-18*)

A. The Day of the Lord Is Sure to Happen (3:1-10)
  • Peter reminds readers of true teaching (3:1-2).
    ▶ Given by prophets.
    ▶ Given by true apostles.
  • False teachers will doubt God's final plan (3:3-4).
  • False teachers doubt God's action in the past (3:5-7).
  • The human view of time is not God's view of time (3:8).
  • God delays judgment because of His love, not because He is slow (3:9).
  • *"Like a thief"* — suddenly. Humans cannot predict when Christ will come (*3:10*).

Key Word
Day of the Lord: In the Old Testament, the day of the Lord is a time when God will come with judgment or blessing (See *Amo. 5:18-20; Joe. 1:15*). In the New Testament, the day of the Lord is also a day of redemption when Christ comes again to bring in the new heaven and new earth (See *Eph. 4:20; 1 Cor. 1:8; 2 Cor. 1:14*).

B. The Day of the Lord is a Call to Godliness (*3:11-16*)
  • *"What manner of persons"* — The purpose of prophecy teaching is not to answer our questions. The purpose is to change our lives (*3:11*).
  • *"Look forward and hastening"* — Godly living will lead others to repentance (*3:12*).

  "So then, dear friends, since you are looking forward to this, make every effort to be found spotless, blameless and at peace with him" (3:14).

NOTES

- *"Found by Him ..."* — Believers have peace with God through the death of Christ (See *Rom. 5:1*). However, they may displease God. Peter urges godly living to please God (*3:14*).
- *"Dear brother Paul"* — Peter recognizes Paul as an apostle with authority. Peter validates Paul's writings as Scripture equal to the Old Testament and in harmony with Paul's claims of apostolic authority (*Rom. 1:1; 1 Cor. 2:13; Gal. 1:1*).

C. Guard Against Error (*3:17-18*)

"...but grow in the grace and knowledge of our Lord and Savior Jesus Christ" (*3:18*).

- A deeper experience in knowledge of the Lord usually comes with a greater understanding and appreciation of grace.

Suggestions for Preaching From *2 Peter*

- How does real faith show in faithful behavior?
- How can believers recognize false teachers?
- How does knowing Christ will return affect our lives now?

Chapter Fifteen
The Letters of John

The author of the *Gospel of John* also wrote the three letters of John. The writer does not identify himself, but the writing style is much like the *Gospel of John*. Also, in the opening verses, the author calls himself an eyewitness to Christ's life.

John died at the end of the first century. The last book he wrote was *Revelation*. He wrote these three letters shortly before that, probably around AD 90. John's writings are the latest in the New Testament. Most likely he wrote these letters from Ephesus. Irenaeus, a Christian from the second century, said that John lived in Ephesus for a time. The heresy of Gnosticism was growing and coming into the church. John wrote the first letter to help his readers know how to decide if a teaching was false.

What to watch for

Key words: fellowship, love.

John's Two-Part Statements:

John's style in *1 John* is to make a statement in two parts. Often he begins the statement with "if." If one thing is true, then the second thing is true. As you study *1 John*, look up these verses in your Bible and make a list of "If … then" statements in the book of *1 John*. What do you learn about John's message from these verses? What other two-part statements can you find in *1 John*?

"If"	"Then"
1:5	1:10
1:6	2:1
1:7	2:15
1:8	2:29
1:9	3:20-21
5:15	5:16

Tip: Open your Bible to *1 John* so you can follow the readings.

1. Introduction: The Message of Eternal Life (*1:1-4*)

    A. John Is an Eyewitness to Jesus Christ (*1:1-2*)

    B. John Writes So Readers Will Know the Truth (*1:3-4*)

NOTES

2. Fellowship with God (*1:5–2:11*)

A. <u>Principles for Fellowship with God</u> (*1:5–2:2*)
- We can have fellowship with God (*1:5-7*).
  ▶ As light and darkness do not go together, so sin and fellowship with God do not go together.
  ▶ False teachers said sin did not matter, because God is spiritual and God saves us. John says sin breaks fellowship with God.

Key Word
Fellowship: This means to share things in common. We have fellowship with God when we participate in the grace of God and salvation through Christ. Fellowship with each other grows from sharing the grace of God and reflects the character of God.

- We have a sinful nature (*1:8-9*).
  ▶ False teachers said they were not sinful because they had special knowledge.
  ▶ John says we do have a sinful nature, but God forgives sin (See *Rom. 3:24-26*).
- We sin in our actions (*1:10–2:2*).
  ▶ False teachers said they did not sin in their daily lives.
  ▶ John says we do sin in our actions, but Jesus Himself is our advocate with God (See *5:10*). If we say we don't sin, then we deny God's Word and that Word has found no place in our heart.

Why do you think people today deny that they sin?

B. <u>Principles for Knowing God</u> (*2:3-11*)
- Obedience: Keeping God's commands shows that we know Him (*2:3-6*).
  ▶ Actions must match up with words.
  ▶ *"Perfected"* — This word means "maturity" or "completeness," rather than living a perfect life and never sinning (*2:5*).
  ▶ This means either that God's love for the believer is complete when the believer obeys, or that our love for God is complete when it shows in obedience.
- Love: the test of obedience (*2:7-11*).
  ▶ "From the beginning" — The command to love is basic to teaching the readers already knew (*2:7; see Lev. 19:18; Mat. 22:39-40*).
  ▶ The command has new meaning because Christ showed us love in His obedience on the cross (*2:8; see Joh. 13:34-35*).
  ▶ Living in the light of Christ means living in love toward each other (*2:9-11*).

Key Word

Love: In five chapters, John uses forms of the word "love" 46 times.[71] He stresses the connection between true faith and love in action. Because we know God's love, we can show love to others.

NOTES

3. The Reason for the Letter (*2:12-27*)

    A. <u>John Writes to Believers of All Ages</u> (*2:12-14*)
- *"Little children"* — a term of affection for all the readers (*2:12*).
- *"Fathers"* and *"young men"* — levels of spiritual maturity.

    B. <u>The Christian's Relationship with the World</u> (*2:15-17*)
- *"World"* — the evil influences that keep us apart from God.
- Loving the world does not go with loving God.
  - ▶ *"Lust of the flesh"* — inner desires of our sinful nature.
  - ▶ *"Lust of the eyes"* — temptation that come through what we see.
  - ▶ *"Pride of life"* — being proud of worldly position.

Use your own words to explain the Christian's relationship with the world.

    C. <u>False Teachers Denied that Jesus is the Christ</u> (*2:18-23*)
- *"Last hour"* — the period that began with Christ's coming. God is in the final stages of His plan for salvation (*2:18*).
- *"Antichrists"* — false teachers who wanted to take the place of Christ. John spoke against them in this letter (*2:18-19*).
- *"Anointing"* — The Holy Spirit, who comes from God and Christ and makes the believer able to know the truth (*2:20*).

    D. <u>Abide in God's Word and Stay with the Truth</u> (*2:24-27*)
- *"Which you heard from the beginning"* — the true Gospel that the apostles preached (*2:24*).
- *"Anointing"* — another reference to the Holy Spirit, who teaches in the believer's life (*2:27*).

4. God's Righteousness (*2:28–4:6*)

    A. <u>Christ's Future Appearing</u> (*2:28–3:3*)
- *"Born of God"* — Children of God will have the righteousness of God (*2:29*).

"Behold what manner of love the Father has bestowed on us, that we should be called children of God!...Beloved, now we are children of God" (*3:1-2*).

NOTES

- *"Be like him"* — Believers will have a resurrection body and be free from sin (*3:2*).
- *"When He is revealed"* — The Christian hope focuses on the return of Christ.

B. <u>The Difference Between Right and Wrong Is Clear</u> (*3:4-10*)
- In the past, Christ came to take away sin (*3:8*).
- Sin is possible in the believer's life, but a habit of sin is inconsistent with being a child of God (*3:9*).
- People are children of God or children of the devil, how we live demonstrates who we really are (*3:10*).

C. <u>Children of God Put Love Into Action</u> (*3:11-15*)
- Cain was a child of the devil. He did not act with love, but with hatred (*3:11-12*).
- Love is proof of moving from the rule of death to the rule of life. Cain hated his brother. We can love (*3:13-15*).

D. <u>Love Shows We Belong to Christ, Not the World</u> (*3:16-24*)

"This is how we know what love is: Jesus Christ laid down his life for us. And we ought to lay down our lives for our brothers…Dear children, let us not love with words or tongue but with actions and in truth" (*3:16-18*).

- Sacrifice is the heart of love. God does not call everyone to sacrifice physical life. He does call us to take action for the sake of others (*3:18-19*).
- *"God is greater than our hearts"* — God knows our hearts, even when we feel we fall short. He knows our inner motives (*3:20-21*).
- Faith and love go together (*3:22-24*).

John stresses that Jesus is God. Make a list of the verses in 1 John that point this out.

E. <u>Test New Teachings</u> (*4:1-6*)
- *"Spirit"* — a person may teach from the Holy Spirit or under the influence of the devil. Believers must know the difference (*4:1*).
- True Christian teaching always says that Jesus is God in the flesh, sent by God for salvation (*4:2-3*).

"You are from God, little children, and have overcome them, because He who is in you is greater than he who is in the world" (*4:4*).

- Believers have the Holy Spirit. He helps us know the truth (*4:4-6*; see *Joh.14:17*).

5. God's Love Takes Action Through Us (*4:7–5:13*)   NOTES

A. <u>Love Shows We Have a Relationship With God</u> (*4:7-16*)

"Beloved, let us love one another, for love is of God; and everyone who loves is born of God and knows God. He who does not love does not know God, for God is love" (*4:7-8*).

- Love begins in God Himself (*4:7-8*).
- God sent His Son to show His love in action toward us (*4:9-11*).
- God's love keeps on working in us as we love one another (*4:12*).
- Love is how we know we live in God (*4:13-16*).
  - ▶ The Spirit tells us we have fellowship with God because of our salvation (*4:13*).
    - ▷ Because of the Spirit, we confess Christ is Lord. Because of the Spirit, we love.
    - ▷ Belief and love are proof of the Spirit in us.
  - ▶ This is the core of the Gospel. God sent His Son to be the Savior. Anyone who believes now has fellowship with God (*4:14-15*).
  - ▶ We live in God's love, not under the rule of worldly values (*4:16*).

B. <u>Love for God and Love for Others</u> (*4:17–5:5*)
- *"Boldness in the day of judgment"* — The person who lives in love will not be ashamed when Christ returns (*4:17*; see *Joh. 15:9-17*).
- *"Perfect love"* — a mature understanding of God's love (*4:18-19*).

"By this we know that we love the children of God, when we love God and keep His commandments. For this is the love of God, that we keep His commandments" (*5:2-3*).

- We love others in response to God's love for us (*5:19-21*).

C. <u>God's Witness that Jesus Is the Christ</u> (*5:6-13*)
- *"Came by water and blood"* — Water symbolizes Jesus' baptism. Blood represents Jesus' death (*5:6*).
  - ▶ Jesus' ministry began with His baptism and ended with His death.
  - ▶ The Father, Son and Holy Spirit all say the same thing (*5:7-8*).
  - ▶ God's testimony is greater than human testimony (*5:9*).
- The testimony: *"God has given us eternal life, and this life is in His Son"* (*5:10*).
  - ▶ The testimony leads to belief (*5:10*).
  - ▶ We do not earn eternal life. God gives eternal life as a gift (*5:11-13*; see *Rom. 6:23*).

6. Prayer and Affirmation (*5:14-21*)

A. <u>Pray According to God's Will</u> (*5:14-17*)

This includes praying for someone who has fallen into sin.

NOTES B. <u>Remember Key Thoughts</u> (*5:18-21*)
- We know Christ keeps those who are born of God (*5:18*).
- We know our spiritual life begins in God (*5:19*).
- We know Christ came so we can know God (*5:20*).
- Fellowship with the true God does not go with worshiping anything false (*5:21*).

Suggestions for Preaching From *1 John*

- Explore John's teaching about sin and forgiveness in the Christian's life.

- Identify how John uses the concept of love in his writings in ways that apply to the daily life of believers.

- Explore the ways we treat others and how this reflects our relationship with God.

—— 2 JOHN ——

The second letter of John answers the question, "Who is Jesus?"

What to watch for

Key word: truth

Tip: Open your Bible to *2 John* so you can follow the readings.

1. Greeting to the "Elect Lady" (*1-3*)

This may be a real person. This may be a way of speaking to the local Church. Regardless, the focus is on truth.

Key Word
Truth: John uses this word five times in the opening verses. He gets right to the point: Watch out for false teaching that changes or manipulates the truth about who Jesus is.

2. Live in the Truth (*4-11*)

A. <u>Walk in Truth and Love</u> (*4-6*)
- *"Walking in truth"* — having a real relationship with God (*4*). As God commanded these Christians, they have been teaching their children to have a real relationship with the Lord.
- *"Love one another"* — Even when writing to teach about those who are against him, John stresses love. Love is obedience to God (*5;* see *1 Joh. 2:7-8*).

- *"From the beginning"* — This is John's way to summarize the true Gospel given by the apostles who knew Jesus (*5-6;* see *1 Joh. 2:7*).

   B. Be Careful About "Deceivers" (*7-11*)
      - *"Confess Jesus Christ"* — Anyone who does not teach that Jesus is God in human flesh is not teaching the truth (*7;* see *1 Joh. 4:2-3*).
      - *"Full reward"* — Faithfulness to God brings future reward (*8;* see *Mar. 9:31; 10:29-30; Luk. 19:16-19; Heb. 11:26*).
      - *"Transgresses," "does not abide"* — Some false teachers, Gnostics, believed they had greater spiritual knowledge than the apostles.
      - Belief that Jesus is God is an essential doctrine (*9*).
      - *"Shares in evil deeds"*—John warns against giving food and shelter to false teachers (*10-11*).

3. Closing (*12-13*)

There is unusual joy when we as believers are able to walk consistently with the Lord and be together face to face.

Suggestions for Preaching From *2 John*

- How can Christians guard against false teaching about who Jesus is?

—— 3 JOHN ——

John writes to shows approval to Gaius, who supported the messengers John sent.

Tip: Open your Bible to *3 John* so you can follow the readings.

1. Greeting to Gaius (*1-4*)

Gaius held to the truth (*3*). As a result this brings joy to John (*4*). There is no greater joy than to know that the physical children and spiritual children you raised are walking with the Lord.

2. Gaius's Responsibility (*5-12*)

   A. Gaius Supports Other Believers (*5-8*)
      - *"Whatever you do for the brethren"* — Church members gave shelter and support to missionaries who traveled (*5;* see *2 Joh. 10*).
      - *"Worthy of God"* — The people Gaius supported told about his acts of love (*6*).

NOTES
- *"Become fellow workers"* — When we support the ministry of other people, we share in the work (*7-8*).

    B. <u>Diotrephes Led Harshly</u> (*9-11*)
- *"Loves to have the preeminence"* — This leader controlled the church for his own purposes (*9*).
- *"If I come"* — John plans to talk to Diotrephes in person. This leader has been speaking against John and not receiving the messengers John sends (*10*). Some preachers consider other preachers to be threats to their ministries rather than coworkers.
- *"Does what is good"* — Actions prove commitment to God (*11;* see *1 Joh. 3:4-9*).

    C. <u>Demetrius Is a Good Example</u> (*12*)
- *"Good testimony"* — He has a good reputation.
- *"From the truth"* — His life showed the Gospel at work in him.

3. Closing (*13-14*)

Jesus taught us to make friends for eternity around the Good News. John learned well. He had many friends.

Suggestions for Preaching From *3 John*

- How does hospitality show faithfulness to God?

Chapter Sixteen
Jude

Jude is most likely the brother of James. This means he was a half-brother to Jesus. Jesus' half-brothers are named in Matthew 13:55: James, Joseph, Simon and Judas (Jude). We are not sure where Jude's first readers were. They were Christians, but they may have been Jewish Christians, Gentile Christians or both. Jude does not mention where his readers were. False teachers said that being saved by grace meant it did not matter if Christians sinned. Jude wrote to warn readers about these false teachers. Their teaching turned into Gnosticism. This philosophy teaches that the soul is trapped in the body. Only the soul is spiritual. Humans may do anything they want with the body because it is not spiritual. Christians have true knowledge and do not have to worry about sins in the body. As apostles, Paul and Peter both wrote to correct this false teaching. Jude also wrote with this purpose. Although Jude was not an apostle, he was a church leader.

Tip: Open your Bible to *Jude* so you can follow the readings.

1. Greeting (*1-2*)

Again the word called is used of believers.

2. The Danger of False Teachers (*3-4*)

- A. <u>Jude Changed the Subject of His Letter</u> (*3*)
    - *"Diligent to write"* — He planned to write a general letter (*3*).
    - *"Found it necessary"* — Specific events made him change the subject (*3*).
    - *"Contend earnestly for the faith"* — Jude writes to defend the Christian teachings of the apostles (*3*; see *1 Cor. 11:1; 15:3-8*).

- B. <u>The Reason for the Change of Subject Was False Teachers</u> (*4*)
    - *"Certain men have crept in"* — False teachers have come into the church.
    - *"Marked out for this condemnation"* — (*4*).
        - ▶ This may mean that the Old Testament spoke against ungodly people.
        - ▶ Or, it might mean judgment was going to fall on the false teachers.[72]
    - *"Turn the grace of our God into lewdness"* — These false teachers lived in immoral ways.
        - ▶ Gnostics taught that humans could sin freely because God will forgive all by His grace.
        - ▶ Other Gnostics taught that human sin shows more of God's grace.
    - *"Deny the only Lord"* — The false teachers rejected Christ's authority as their master.

NOTES

3. God Judges Sin (5-7)

A. <u>God Judged Unbelieving Israel</u> (5)
- *"You once knew"* — Jude tells the readers something they already were aware of. They forgot to guard against false teachers.
- *"Destroyed those who did not believe"* — God promised to give His people the land of Canaan. The people did not believe.
  - ▶ The generation who did not believe died in the desert (See *Num. 14:29-30; Deu. 1:32-36; 1 Cor. 10:1-5*).

Why does Jude talk about false teaching and judgment in the same letter?

B. <u>God Judged Angels</u> (6).
- It is unclear who these angels are.
  - ▶ They are not God's holy angels.
  - ▶ They must be angels who followed Satan's rebellion against God. They seem to be of a different rank, deserving of even more specific punishment.
- The main point is that the angels rebelled and God punished them (See *2 Pet. 2:4*). These demonic spirits are subject to the condemnation of the Lord. Some scholars feel that these are the ones who are seen in *Genesis 6:1-8*.

C. <u>God Judged Sodom and Gomorrah</u> (7)
- *"Strange flesh"* — homosexual activity
- *"Set forth as an example"* — God judged the cities with fire from heaven (See *Gen. 19:24*).

4. The Wickedness of the False Teachers (8-16)

A. <u>The False Teachers Reject Authority</u> (8-10)
- *"Dreamers"* — The false teachers lost their connection to the truth.
  - ▶ *"Defile the flesh"* — probably homosexual activity.
  - ▶ *"Reject authority"* — did not submit to people in authority in the church.
  - ▶ *"Speak evil"* — not only rejected, but spoke against people in authority.
- *"Michael...in contending with the devil"* — (9).
  - ▶ This is based on a writing called *The Testament of Moses* written in the first century.
  - ▶ *Daniel 10:13* may be the battle between Satan and Michael the Angel (Israel's special guardian).

▶ Jude uses this story as an example of the pride of the false teachers.
▶ Even Michael, the highest ranking angel, did not speak against his enemy.
▷ Michael left the judgment to God.
- *"These speak evil"* — In contrast to Michael, the false teachers say whatever they like about authority (*10*).

B. <u>The False Teachers Sin in Several Ways</u> (*11-13*)

"Woe to them! For they have gone in the way of Cain, have run greedily in the error of Balaam for profit, and perished in the rebellion of Korah" (*11*).

- Three Old Testament examples of rebellion against authority. All these people faced God's judgment (*11; see Gen. 4:3-8; Num. 31:16; 16:1-3, 31-35*).
- Jude uses metaphors to describe the false teachers. What do these images say about false teachers? (*12-13*).

Beside each metaphor, write what you think Jude means.

- *"spots at your love feasts"*

- *"clouds without water"*

- *"autumn trees without fruit"*

- *"raging waves of the sea"*

- *"wandering stars"*

- The false teachers put on a big show, but they are empty of truth.

C. <u>The False Teachers Face Judgment</u> (*14-16*)
- *"Seventh from Adam"* — Jude quotes from another book, *The Book of Enoch*.
▶ Most likely this book was not written until the first century, rather than in Old Testament times.

NOTES

▶ Jude uses this example to point to Christ's Second Coming and judgment of the wicked.[73]
- *"Flattering people to gain advantage"* — The false teachers serve themselves, not God.

5. Christians, Be Alert! (*17-23*)

A. <u>Pay Attention to the Apostles</u> (*17-18*)
- *"Words spoken before by the apostles"* — Jude reminds his readers that the apostles have authority (*17*).
- *"Mockers in the last time"* — The apostles warned about false teachers. It should be no surprise when they appear (*18;* see *Act. 20:29; 1 Tim. 4:1-2; 2 Tim. 3:1-5; 2 Pet. 2:1-3; 3:2-3*).

Why do you think Jude stresses the words of the apostles?

B. <u>Watch Out for False Teachers</u> (*19*)
- Gnostics claimed to have special knowledge.
- Jude says they do not even have the Spirit. Without the Spirit they are not saved (See *Rom. 8:9*).

C. <u>Grow in God's Grace</u> (*20-21*)

"But you, beloved, building yourself up on your most holy faith, praying in the Holy Spirit, keep yourselves in the love of God, looking for the mercy of our Lord Jesus Christ unto eternal life" (*20-21*).

- Being led by the Holy Spirit in prayer is in contrast to the false teachers, who are led by their own corrupt minds (*Eph. 5:18*).
- Jude points the readers back to the true Gospel.

D. <u>Care for Others</u> (*22-23*)
- Show mercy to people in need in the church.
- Consider wisely how to help each other grow spiritually.
- Stay away from sin.

6. Blessing God (*24-25*)

"Now to Him who is able to keep you from stumbling, and to present you faultless before the presence of His glory with exceeding joy, to God our Savior, Who alone is wise, be glory and majesty, dominion and power, both now and forever" (24-25).

This has become one of the greatest blessings and prayers in church history. It expresses part of God's character and our need.

Suggestions for Preaching from *Jude*

- Explore how false teachers are dangerous to the Christian's spiritual life.

NOTES

Chapter Seventeen
Revelation

The book of *Revelation* is like nothing else in the New Testament. It is an example of "apocalyptic" literature. Apocalyptic writings are full of symbols. *Revelation* follows this style. Other examples in the Bible are portions of *Daniel, Ezekiel and Zechariah*. Apocalyptic literature was also popular outside of the Bible.

The writer of *Revelation* is John, the disciple of Jesus in the Gospels. This is the same John who wrote the *Gospel of John* and the letters of *1, 2* and *3 John*. Historical sources tell us that John lived in Ephesus in the late first century. From this city, John ministered to other cities in Asia (modern Turkey). Under the rule of Emperor Domitian, Christians suffered persecution because they would not worship the Roman emperor. As punishment for his Christian activities, John was a prisoner on the island of Patmos (*1:9*). Patmos is about sixty miles away from Ephesus in the Aegean Sea. The book of *Revelation* records the visions and messages John received while he was on Patmos.

John wrote to encourage Christians to stand firm against emperor worship. The theme of *Revelation* is God's control of history. God has already defeated Satan. One day Christ will return. Human history will come to an end. At that time, the wicked will be destroyed. God's people will enter eternal glory.

What to watch for

Key Words: blessed, angel, seven, tribulation.

Key Concept: Antichrist.

Tip: Open your Bible to *Revelation* so you can follow the readings.

1. Introduction (*1:1-20*)

    A. Opening (*1:1-3*)
- *"Of Jesus Christ"* — This can mean the writing comes from Jesus or is about Jesus, or both (*1:1*).
- Jesus Christ sent an angel to John. Jesus is the divine source of the vision. John is the human who records it.

Key Word
Blessed: *Revelation* contains seven words of blessing (see *1:3; 13:14; 16:15; 19:9; 22:7; 22:14*). "Blessed" means more than happy in human terms. Believers are "happy" because they share in what God is doing. This includes the events of the end of time.

    B. Greetings and Praise (*1:4-8*)
- *"Seven churches"* — churches in the Roman province of Asia (*1:4*). Most likely the entire letter of *Revelation* was sent to each church.

NOTES

- *"Seven spirits"* — may refer to the angels of the seven churches mentioned in *chapters 2* and *3*. It may also mean a "sevenfold" Spirit; that is, the Holy Spirit.[74]
- *"Who loved us…"* — John summarizes the work that Christ already did for us (*1:5-6*).
- *"Coming with clouds"* — points to Christ's return (*1:7*).
- *"Alpha and Omega"* — the first and last letters of the Greek alphabet. God is the beginning and the end of human history.
  ▶ John also refers to Jesus as the "Word," the ultimate communication of God to man (*Joh. 1:1*).

C. <u>The Son of Man and the Churches</u> (*1:9-20*)
- *"In the Spirit"* — John sees a vision of Christ. Christ gives him a message for the churches (*1:9-11*).
- *"Seven golden lampstands"* — represents the seven churches (*1:12*).
- *"One like the Son of Man"* — Christ (*1:13-16*; see *Dan. 7:13*). Jesus used this title for Himself (*Mat. 20:28*).
  ▶ *"Garment," "golden band"* — Jesus is dressed like a high priest (*1:13*; see *Exo. 18:4; 29:5*).
  ▶ *"White like wool," "white as snow"* — (*1:14*). The white appearance is similar to the "Ancient of Days" in *Dan. 7:9* and Christ at the time of the Transfiguration in *Mat. 17:2*.
  ▶ *"Flame of fire"* — righteousness and judgment (*1:14*; see *Dan. 10:6; 1 Cor. 3:13*).[75]
  ▶ *"Seven stars"* — the seven angels of the seven churches (see *1:20; 1:16*).

Key Word
Angel: John uses the word "angel" 67 times in the book of Revelation. Angels surround God's throne and fill heaven with songs of praise (*5:11; 7:11*). They also play a key role in the events of the final time before Christ returns by giving visions and announcing judgment (*1:1; 9:1, 13; 11:15; 14:15, 17; 15:1; 18:1; 19:17; 20:1*).

- John responds to the vision in worship. Jesus speaks to John (*1:17-20*).
  ▶ *"He who lives"* — the living God of the Old Testament (*1:18*; see *Jos. 3:10; Psa. 42:2; 84:2*).
  ▶ *"Keys of Hades and of Death"* — Christ has all authority (*1:18*).
  ▶ *"What you have seen"* — the vision of *chapter 1*.
  ▶ *"What is now"* — the condition of the seven churches in *Rev. 2* and *3*.
  ▶ *"What will take place later"* — future events of *Rev. 4–22*.

2. Seven Letters to Seven Churches (*2:1–3:22*)

A. <u>The Church in Ephesus</u> (*2:1-7*)
- Ephesus was a major trade and religious city in the region.
- *"I know your works"* — (*2:2*).
  ▶ This phrase appears in each of the seven letters (*2:9; 2:13; 3:1; 3:8; 3:15*).
  ▶ God knows the true condition of hearts and churches.

- Christians at Ephesus had worked hard. However, they neglected love for each other (*2:4*).
- Christ calls for repentance (*2:5*).
- *"Nicolaitans"* — a group within the church following false teaching (*2:6*). The church in Ephesus rightly turned away from this false teaching. The New Testament does not record what this false teaching was.
- *"Him who overcomes"* — The challenge to continue to obey appears in each of the seven letters (see *2:11, 17, 26; 3:5, 12, 21*). Jesus calls believers to live obedient lives even when they face troubles.

At the end of each letter to the seven churches, we read, "He that has an ear, let him hear what the Spirit says to the churches." What do you think this phrase means?

What lesson do you see for the church today in these words to the church in Ephesus? Discuss.

Key Word
Seven: John uses the number seven 52 times in the book of *Revelation*. He mentions seven beatitudes, seven churches, seven spirits, seven golden lampstands, seven stars, seven seals, seven horns, seven eyes, seven trumpets, seven thunders, seven signs, seven crowns, seven plagues, seven golden bowls, seven hills, seven kings and other items. The number seven is a symbol for completeness.[76]

B. <u>The church in Smyrna</u> (*2:8-11*)
- Smyrna was one of the first cities to worship the Roman emperor.
- *"Tribulation"* — Christians in Smyrna faced deep troubles and poverty, but spiritually they were rich (*2:9-10*).
- *"Crown of life"* — In Greek athletic events, the winner wore a wreath of victory (*2:10;* see *Jam. 1:12*). Believers who stay faithful will enjoy life in God's kingdom.
- Death contrasts with life. Only eternal life matters.

What lesson do you see for the church today in the letter to Smyrna? Discuss.

NOTES

C. The Church in Pergamos (*2:12-17*)
- Pergamos was the center of worshiping the emperor in Asia.
- *"Balak"* — (*2:14;* see *Num. 22–25*). Balak hired Balaam to lead Israel away from God.
- Some in Pergamos followed false teachers, especially in worshiping idols and taking part in sexual immorality (See Act. 15:20).
- *"Sword of My mouth"* — symbol of divine judgment (*2:16;* see *1:16*).

What lesson do you see for the church today in the letter to Pergamos? Discuss.

D. The Church in Thyatira (*2:18-29*)
- Thyatira was a center for many kinds of businesses.
- *"Jezebel"* — A woman in the church defied loyalty to God. She tolerated pagan worship for Christians. This is a misuse of Christian freedom (See *2 Cor. 8:4*).
- *"Children"* — This woman is the spiritual mother of anyone who misuses Christian freedom (*2:22*).
- *"Depths of Satan"* — Gnosticism was a major kind of false teaching. This philosophy said that humans must experience evil in order to defeat Satan (*2:24*).[77]

What lesson do you see for the church today in the letter to Thyatira? Discuss.

E. The Church in Sardis (*3:1-6*)
- Sardis was a city of great wealth and fame. It was built on a hill where five roads crossed.
- *"Seven spirits"* — may be the Holy Spirit (*3:1*).
- This church was overconfident. They were not watchful spiritually (*3:2-3*).
- *"Who have not defiled their garments"* — Some Christians in Sardis did turn away from sin and live in righteous ways (*3:4*).
- *"Book of Life"* — the list of those who believe and are citizens of God's kingdom (*3:5;* see *Exo. 32:32-33; Rev. 13:8; 17:8; 20:12; 20:15; 21:27*).[78]

What lesson do you see for the church today in the letter to Sardis? Discuss.

NOTES

F. The Church in Philadelphia (*3:7-13*)
- Philadelphia's name means "brotherly love." Jesus finds no fault in this church.
- This church was small but faithful (*3:8-10*).
- *"Synagogue of Satan"* — Those who claimed to be Jews because of circumcision. They are not the ones with true faith (*3:9; see Rom. 2:28-29*).
- *"Keep you from"* — This phrase can mean "keep you from undergoing" or "keep you through" (*3:10*).[79]
- *"Hour of trial"* — This is the final period of testing in the world before (*3:10*).
- Christ's promise to come soon is encouragement to keep on being faithful (*3:11*).

What lesson do you see for the church today in the letter to Philadelphia? Discuss.

G. The Church in Laodicea (*3:14-22*)
- Laodicea was one of the richest business centers of the world.
- The church was wealthy and did not see its own spiritual poverty (*3:17*).
- *"Lukewarm"* — The church was not hot enough to bring spiritual healing, as hot spring waters aid physical healing. And it was not cold enough to bring refreshment.
- They were proud of wealth, clothing businesses and eye medicine (*3:18*). What Christ gives spiritually is worth more than what they were proud of.
- *"Stand at the door"* — Jesus is trying to get into His own church.

What lesson do you see for the church today in the letter to Laodicea? Discuss.

NOTES

3. Visions of the End of Time (*4:1–22:5*)

A. The Heavenly Throne Room (*4:1–5:14*)
- The throne in heaven (*4:1-11*).
  - ▶ *"After these things"* — shows a change to a new section or a new vision. John now sees God's throne in heaven (*4:1-2*).
  - ▶ *"Come up here"* — Some see here the rapture, or removal of the church from the earth (*4:1*).[80]
  - ▶ *"In the Spirit"* — high level of spiritual awareness because of the power of the Holy Spirit (*4:2*).

  "… and behold, a throne set in heaven, and One sat on the throne. And He who sat there was like a jasper and a sardius stone in appearance; and there was a rainbow around the throne, in appearance like an emerald" (*4:2b-3*).

  - ▶ John uses the word "throne" 47 times in *Revelation*. This is far more than any other New Testament writer. The throne is a symbol of power and authority (See *Psa. 47:8*).
  - ▶ *"Elders"* — representing all believers, or, a kind of angels worshiping God (*4:4*).
    - ▷ Some see the elders as the church removed from earth and now worshiping in heaven. In this view, the church does not suffer the great tribulation on earth.
    - ▷ The number 24 may reflect the 12 tribes of Israel in the Old Testament and the 12 apostles of the New Testament.[81]
  - ▶ *"Lightnings, thunderings, and voices"* — symbols of the power of God (*4:5; see Exo. 19:16-19; Psa. 18:12-15; 77:18*).
  - ▶ *"Four living creatures"* — a high level of angels who guard the throne (*4:6; see Eze. 10:1-10* for a similar description of cherubim).
    - ▷ *"Lion," "calf," "face like a man," "flying eagle"* — The creatures may represent all of creation.
    - ▷ All of creation shares in God's redemption.
  - ▶ The four living creatures and twenty-four elders worship God, who sits on the throne (*4:7*).
- The scroll with seven seals and the triumphant Lamb (*5:1-14*).
  - ▶ *"Seven seals"* — No one can read the scroll until someone opens all seven seals (*5:1*).
  - ▶ No one on heaven or earth could open the seals (*5:2-4*).
  - ▶ *"Lion of the tribe of Judah, the Root of David"* — Messianic titles for Jesus Christ (*5:5; see Gen. 49:8-10; Isa. 11:1, 10; Rom. 15:12; Heb 7:14*).
  - ▶ *"Lamb"* — John uses a word for "lamb" that no other New Testament writer uses.
    - ▷ Jesus is the sacrifice for sin (See *Isa. 43:7, Joh. 1:29*).
    - ▷ Jesus is also the conqueror. The lamb as a military hero comes from apocalyptic writings.
    - ▷ The horn is a symbol of power. Seven horns is a symbol of complete power.

▶ *"New song"* — In the Old Testament, God's people sang songs to celebrate God's actions or blessing (5:9; see *Psa. 33:3; 96:1; 144:9*).
▶ This is a picture of worship and praise that no one else deserves. Only Christ deserves this praise from every creature (*5:10-14*).

NOTES

Major Images of *Revelation*: As you read and study John's vision of the end of time, write down your thoughts about what these images and symbols mean. Base your answers on what you read in the book of *Revelation*.

Thrones and elders (*Chapter 4*):

Scroll (*Chapter 5*):

Seals, Trumpets, Bowls (*Chapters 6–16*):

Woman and Dragon (*Chapter 12*):

Beasts (*Chapter 13*):

Scarlet Woman (*Chapter 17*):

Bride of Christ (*Chapter 19*):

B. The Lamb Opens the Seven Seals (*6:1-8:1*)
- The first six seals prepare for the day of God's wrath (*6:1-17*).
  ▶ **Seal 1:** the White Horse — White is a symbol of military victory (*6:1-2*; see *Zec. 1:8-17; 6:1-8*).
    ▷ Some take this as an image of Christ.
    ▷ More likely it symbolizes victory.[82]
  ▶ **Seal 2:** the Red Horse — This horse is a symbol of bloodshed (*6:3-4*).
    ▷ Conquest comes from the outside.
    ▷ This bloodshed comes from the inside — men slaying each other.
  ▶ **Seal 3:** the Black horse — This horse is a symbol of famine (*6:5-6*).
    ▷ The scales show that food costs a great deal of money.
    ▷ A denarius was a day's wage. This only bought enough food for one person.
  ▶ **Seal 4:** the Pale Horse — This horse is a symbol of Death. Death results from military conquest, bloodshed and famine (*6:7-8*).
  ▶ **Seal 5:** the souls under the altar — This is a symbol of martyrs who died because of their faith in God (*6:9-11*).

NOTES

- ▷ In the Old Testament, blood was poured at the bottom of the altar (See *Exo. 19:12*).
- ▷ *"White robe"* — a symbol of overcoming trials (See *3:5*).
- ▶ **Seal 6:** the great earthquake — This is a symbol of the destruction of the earth (*6:12-17*).
  - ▷ Prophetic and apocalyptic writers often picture the end of the earth as cosmic disasters (See *Isa. 2:19; Hag. 2:6; Joe. 2:31; Mar. 13:25-26*).
  - ▷ These events strike fear in the hearts of humans.
  - ▷ The day of wrath is coming soon (See *Zep. 1:14-18; Nah. 1:6; Mal. 3:2*).
- • Interlude: great multitudes in white robes (*7:1-17*).
  - ▶ The sealing of 144,000 — (*7:1-8*).
    - ▷ *"four angels," "four corners," four winds"* — This is a picture of how God is holding back the destruction that will come in the judgment (*7:1*).
    - ▷ *"seal"* — Before the judgment starts, God puts a sign of ownership on His servants. God will protect His people in the judgment (*7:2*).
    - ▷ 144,000 — Some take this as an actual number from the Jewish tribes. In this view, God will protect Israel.[83] Others believe the number is a symbol of believers who live during the great tribulation.[84]
  - ▶ The great multitude — (*7:9-17*).
    - ▷ People who have come through the great tribulation (*7:9* and *7:14*).
    - ▷ *"from every nation ..."* — this may represent people saved during the tribulation because of the ministry of the 144,000, or it may be martyrs.
    - ▷ *"white"* — a symbol of righteousness. Some see this as a sign of martyrs who escaped tribulation by death.[85] (*7:9, 7:14*).
    - ▷ The scene of worship at the throne of God grows more intense.

"Therefore they are before the throne of God, and serve Him day and night in His temple. And He who sits on the throne will be among them. They shall neither hunger anymore nor thirst anymore; the sun shall not strike them, nor any heat; for the Lamb who is in the midst of the throne will shepherd them and lead them to living fountains of waters. And God will wipe away every tear from their eyes" (*7:15-17*)

- • **Seal 7:** silence in heaven (*8:1*).
  - ▶ The final seal on the scroll (*5:1*) is finally opened.
  - ▶ *"Silence in heaven"* — a dramatic pause before the judgments that come in the seven trumpets.

Key Word
Tribulation: This is a time of intense suffering or persecution. In the book of *Revelation* we read about the "great tribulation." This is a time of worldwide rebellion against God and widespread suffering. The great tribulation fulfills the prophecies of *Daniel*

7–12. It will be a time of false christs and false prophets. The great tribulation is part of God's plan to redeem the world and create a new heaven and a new earth.

    C. <u>Seven Trumpets Announce Judgment</u> (*8:2–11:19*)
- An angel throws fire from the altar to the earth to begin the judgments (*8:2-5*).
  - *"Trumpets"* — In the Old Testament, a horn announced important events or time of battle (*8:2;* see *Num. 10:7-9; 1 Kin. 1:34-39; Lev. 25:9*).
  - *"Prayers of the saints"* — The prayers of believers have a part in the judgment of God. The fire from this heavenly offering begins the series of judgments (*8:3-5;* see *4:5*).
- The first six trumpets: greater and greater destruction and woe (*8:6–9:21*).
  - Some believe the judgments of the trumpets come out of the seventh seal. Later, the seven bowls come out of the seventh trumpet. Others believe the seven seals, seven trumpets and seven seals describe the same time period, but more severe each time.
  - **Trumpet 1:** hail and fire mixed with blood (*8:6-7*).
    - *"hail and fire ... mingled with blood"* — the same images as the seventh plague on Egypt (See *Exo. 9:13-15*).
    - *"a third of ..."* — destruction was not complete. This theme repeats throughout the trumpet judgments.
  - **Trumpet 2:** mountain thrown into the sea (*8:8-9*).
    - The first trumpet is a picture of the destruction of land.
    - The second trumpet is a picture of the destruction of sea (See *Exo. 7:20-21*).
  - **Trumpet 3:** the star Wormwood (*8:10-11*).
    - *"Wormword"* — a plant with a strong bitter taste.
    - The waters turn bitter. See *Exo. 15:25* for a story where bitter waters turned sweet.
  - **Trumpet 4:** one-third of the sun, moon and stars struck (*8:12-13*).
    - See *Exo. 10:21-23*. Darkness covered the land.
    - *"Woe, woe, woe"* — refers to the impact of the three judgments of the last three trumpets.
  - **Trumpet 5:** the plague of locusts (*9:1-12*).
    - *"star"* — The star in *8:10* was part of the picture of destruction. This star is a person or a being (*9:1*).
    - *"bottomless pit"* — a place where spirits live, but the key shows it is under God's control (*9:2*).
    - *"locusts"* — (See *Exo. 10:1-20*; also, *Joe. 1:2–2:11*).
    - Their work is torture of human beings.
    - *"who do not have the seal"* — God protects the 144,000 He sealed (*9:4;* see *7:2-4*).
    - *"five months"* — the lifespan of a locust (*9:5-6*).
    - *"Abaddon," "Apollyon"* — This name means "Destruction." (*9:11*).
  - **Trumpet 6:** release of the four angels (*9:13-21*).
    - *"voice"* — This voice of authority belongs to the Lamb (*9:13;* see *5:9*).
    - *"great river Euphrates"* — (*9:14*). This is the eastern boundary

NOTES

163

NOTES

of the land God promised to Abraham (see *Gen. 15:18*). Also, enemies of Israel rose from this region (see *Isa. 8:5-8*).
▷ (*9:15-19*) - Demonic horsemen kill one-third of humans. Some believe this is a literal number. Others believe it means widespread destruction but not complete destruction.
▷ *"did not repent"* — Even with this level of destruction, some refuse to turn to Jesus (*9:20-21;* see *Exo. 7:22; 9:7*, where Pharaoh refused to repent after plagues). The suffering during the tribulation brings a chance to believe and repent (See *Amo. 4:6-11*).

How are the seven seals and seven trumpets similar? Discuss.

- Interlude: the little book and the two witnesses (*10:1–11:14*).
  ▶ The angel tells John to eat a little book (*10:1-11*).

  "I saw still another mighty angel coming down from heaven, clothed with a cloud. And a rainbow was on his head, his face was like the sun, and his feet like pillars of fire" (*10:1*).

  ▷ This angel could be the same angel mentioned in *5:2* and *18:1*. His size is a symbol of God's power.
  ▷ *"little book"* — This is not the scroll mentioned in *5:2*, which was opened in chapters *6–8*.
  ▷ *"seven thunders"* — announcing God's coming judgment (*10:4;* see *8:5; 11:19; 16:18*).
  ▷ *"seal up"*—The voice from heaven said it is not time to reveal what the seven thunders said (*10:4;* see *Dan. 8:26* where prophecies are sealed until the last times).
  ▷ *"mystery of God"* — God has revealed some parts of the mystery in the Bible, but we wait for the end of time to see how God wins the victory. The angel says this time is coming soon (*10:7*).
  ▷ John eats the scroll. Words of judgment make his stomach bitter (*10:9-11*).
  ▶ God gives power to two witnesses (*11:1-14*).
  ▷ *"measure"* — In his vision John measures the earthly temple, which will be destroyed (*11:1;* see *Eze. 40:3-4; Dan. 9:27; Luk. 21:24; 2 The. 2:4*). Measuring is for protection.
  ▷ *"forty-two months"* — the same as 1,260 days and *"a time and times and half a time"* in *12:14*, or three and a half years (*11:3;* see *Dan. 12:6-7, 11-12*). Evil will dominate for three and a half years before the final days of the Antichrist.
  ▷ Two witnesses will preach with God's power (*11:5-6*). They are similar to Elijah (see *1 Kin. 17; Mal. 4:5*) and Moses (see *Exo. 7–11*).

- ▷ At the end of the ministry of the witnesses, the beast comes (*11:7*). This is the first time John mentions the great enemy of God in the final times.
- ▷ The witnesses lie dead in the street for three and a half days. This is a great indignity. Then God raises them and takes them to heaven. In *Revelation* the "great city" often means Rome, but it may also be Jerusalem ("where our Lord was crucified"). The great city also may be a symbol of the world opposed to God.[86]
- ▷ *"second woe"* — Trumpet 6 and the interlude come to an end (*11:14*).
- **Trumpet 7:** loud voices in heaven (*11:15-19*).
  - ▶ The trumpet announces the kingdom of God (*11:15*).
  - ▶ The response in heaven is worship. This song of worship praises God for His judgment and rewards (*11:16-18*).
  - ▶ *"Opened in heaven"* — This is the temple in heaven (*3:12; 7:15; 15:5-8*), not the temple on earth (*11:1*).
    - ▷ *"ark of the covenant"* — The Old Testament chest that was a symbol of the presence of God with His people.
    - ▷ God opens His kingdom to His people (*11:19;* see *Heb. 9:1, 4, 11, 23-28*).

D. <u>Signs Before the Final Judgment</u> (*12:1–14:20*)
- The mother of the future Ruler and the dragon (*12:1-17*).
  - ▶ *"Sign"* — a person or event that points to great significance (*12:1*). Revelation has both divine signs (*12:3; 15:1*) and demonic signs (*13:13-14; 16:14; 19:20*).[87]
  - ▶ *"Woman clothed with the sun"* — Some believe this is Israel (see *Gen. 37:9-11*). Some believe it is Jews who believe in Jesus as Messiah (see *Rev. 12:17*). Some believe it is the church (*12:1*).
    - ▷ The Old Testament uses the image of a woman in travail (See *Isa. 26:16; 66:7-8; Mic. 4:10; Mic. 5:3*).
  - ▶ *"Dragon"* — John identifies the dragon as Satan (*12:4; 12:9*).
  - ▶ *"Male child"* — the Messiah (*12:5;* see *Psa. 2:8-9*).
  - ▶ *"Child snatched," "wilderness."* (*12:5-6*).
    - ▷ God saves the child who will carry out His plan for salvation. His power is greater than the power of Satan. This may represent Christ's ascension to heaven in *Act. 1:9*.
    - ▷ The wilderness is a place of protection (*12:6;* see *Hos. 2:14*).
    - ▷ *"1,260 days"* — equal to the time of the persecution (*12:6;* see *11:1*).
  - ▶ *"War in heaven"* — Michael, the archangel defeats Satan (*12:7-9*).
    - ▷ Michael throws Satan out of heaven and into earth. Earth becomes the place where the devil works (See *Dan. 10:13; 12:1; Jude 9*).
    - ▷ This is a picture of the final victory of God over Satan.
  - ▶ *"Loud voice"* — announces victory (*12:10-11*).
  - ▶ *"Pursued the woman"* — The dragon is furious. He wants the child, who is God's Messiah (*12:13-17*).
    - ▷ *"wings of a great eagle"* — another picture of God's protection (See *Exo. 19:4; Deu. 32:11-12*).
    - ▷ *"time, times and half a time"* — the same length of time that the

NOTES

NOTES

> two witnesses preached (*11:3*), and the beast's authority (*13:5; see also Dan. 7:25; 12:7*).

▷ *"water ... like a flood"* — The earth opened up and saved the woman (*12:16;* see *Num. 16:30-33* for a story of the earth opening up).

▷ *"keep the commandments"* — Satan now turns his fury to believers (*12:17*).

▶ The primary truth of the chapter is because God defeated Satan, Satan takes out his anger on humans. Satan, seeks to harm true believers during this time and ever since the fall.

How do you think these pictures of God's victory over Satan encouraged John's first readers?

How can pictures of God's victory encourage believers now?

- The beasts from the sea and the earth (*13:1-18*).
  ▶ *"Beast rising up out of the sea"* — (*13:1-10*). This image comes from *Daniel 7*, where four beasts come out of the sea.
    ▷ The seven heads and ten horns connect the beast to Satan (*13:1; see 12:3*). The beast receives his power from Satan.
    ▷ The descriptions of leopard, bear and lion connect the beast to the beasts of *Dan. 7:4-6*.
    ▷ *"fatal wound"* — This wound is healed, a sign of the power of the beast. This power persuades people to follow him (*13:3-4*).
    ▷ *"blasphemies"* — humans claiming loyalty and worship over God.
    ▷ The beast has power for three and a half years.
  ▶ *"Beast coming out of the earth"* — (*13:11-18*).
    ▷ Some believe that the first beast represents civil power and the second beast represents religions. Others see the second beast as the personal false prophet (*16:13; 19:20; 20:10*).[88]
    ▷ *"two horns like a lamb"* — he tries to appear gentle (*13:11*).
    ▷ The trinity of evil is the dragon, the first beast and the second beast, or Satan, the Antichrist and the false prophet. They join together to work against God, the Father, Son and Holy Spirit (*13:12*).

- The power of the beast from the earth deceives humans into false worship (*13:14-15*).
- This beast marks humans who must follow him or suffer (*13:16-17*). Receiving or rejecting this mark would be the final test of loyalty.
- *"666"* — The number 7 is the symbol of completeness. The number 6 is just short of 7. It is the symbol of the most powerful man who is not God.[89]

Key Concept

Antichrist: Often we connect this word to the book of *Revelation*. Only John uses this word in the New Testament, but he does not use it in *Revelation*. Rather, he uses it to warn believers in his letters of *1* and *2 John* (*1 Joh. 2:18; 2:22; 4:3; 2 Joh. 7*). John warns of many false prophets who oppose Jesus, and says that the supreme Antichrist will come in the future. The Antichrist deceives humans and works against God on a worldwide scale. Though John does not use the word in *Revelation*, his descriptions in *Rev. 13* fit what he says of the "beast" in his letters when he writes about deception and rebellion.

- The Lamb and the 144,000 (*14:1-5*).
  - *"I looked"* — the scene changes from the beast to the Lamb (*14:1*).
  - *"Mount Zion"* — In the Old Testament, Mount Zion meant the city of Jerusalem. Here it means the heavenly Jerusalem that comes to the new earth in *21:2-3*.
  - The 144,000 have the name of God instead of the mark of the beast (*14:1;* see *7:2-4*).
    - This seems to be the same group as in *chapter 7*, but at a later point in time.
    - These people live through the tribulation. Many Gentiles and Jews will turn to Christ in the end time.[90]
  - *"Voice from heaven"* — (*14:2;* see *1:15; 6:1*).
  - *"New song"* — (*14:3;* see *5:9*). The theme of this song is God's deliverance of those He redeemed.
    - Only those are faithful to God, and not the beast, sing this song (*13:3-4*).
    - *"virgins"* — those who are spiritually loyal (*14:4*).
  - *"Firstfruits"* may mean that more will come to believe in Jesus (*14:4*).

What do you think it means that John keeps hearing a voice or sounds from heaven? See *1:15; 5:9; 6:1; 14:1; 14:15; 19:6*.

NOTES
- The Good News is preached (*14:6-20*).
  - ▶ An angel calls people to repent. There is still time before the final judgment (*14:6-7*).
  - ▶ A second angel announces that Babylon has fallen (*14:8*).
    - ▷ This is the first time John mentions Babylon (See *16:19; 17:5; 18:2, 10, 21*). It becomes the focus of God's judgment.
    - ▷ Some believe "Babylon" refers to Rome, the major world power in the first century that opposed God. Others believe Babylon is a symbol for world leaders under the rule of the Antichrist.[91] (See *17:1–18:24* for a description of the fall of Babylon).
  - ▶ A third angel announces that anyone who worships the beast will face the full strength of God's wrath (*14:9-11; see 6:17; 11:18*).
    - ▷ *"fire and brimstone"* — (*14:11*) See *Psa. 11:6* for the fate of the wicked.
    - ▷ John uses this expression several times (See *19:20; 20:10; 21:8*).
  - ▶ *"Patience of the saints"* — endurance in keeping God's commands (*14:12*).
  - ▶ *"Blessed"* — This is the second blessing, or beatitude, out of seven in *Revelation* (*14:13; see 1:3*).
  - ▶ The image of harvesting the earth is a picture of the final judgment (*14:14-16; see Rev. 19–20* for description).
    - ▷ *"One like the Son of Man"* — the reaper is Jesus Christ (*14:14*).
    - ▷ Christ will judge humankind. A sickle was the tool for a grain harvest (*14:15-16*).
    - ▷ Human history is moving toward the day when Christ will judge.
  - ▶ The grapes of wrath (*14:17-20*).
    - ▷ *"who had power over fire"* — fire often is a symbol of judgment (*14:18; see Lam. 1:13; Mat. 18:8; Luk. 9:54; 2 The. 1:7*).
    - ▷ *"winepress"* — (*14:19-20*). This is a channel where workers trampled grapes with their feet. This caused the juice to flow. Trampling grapes is an Old Testament image of God's wrath (See *Isa. 63:3; Lam. 1:15; Joe. 3:13*).
    - ▷ 1,600 furlongs is almost 200 miles. God crushes evil completely.

E. Seven Bowls of the Wrath of God (*15:1–19:5*)
- The seven angels with the bowls (*15:1-8*).
  - ▶ *"The wrath of God is complete"* — After the angels pour out the bowls of God's wrath, Jesus comes immediately (*15:1; see 19:6-21*).
  - ▶ *"Sea of glass"* — before the throne of God (*15:2; see 4:6*). Mingling with fire means the time for judgment has come.
  - ▶ *"Song of Moses"* — Israel celebrated deliverance from Egypt with a song (*15:3; see Exo. 15:1-18*). Jews sang this song in Sabbath worship. Early Christians sang it at Easter. As the "song of the Lamb" it shows God's deliverance of believers through Jesus Christ.

"Great and marvelous are Your works, Lord God Almighty! Just and true are Your ways, O King of the saints! Who shall not fear You, O Lord, and glorify your name? For You alone are holy. For all nations shall come and worship before You, For Your judgments have been manifested" (*15:3-4*).

- ▶ *"Tabernacle of the testimony"* — This phrase remembers the Law given to Moses and the way God dwelled with His people (*15:5;* see *Exo. 31:18; 32:15*).
- ▶ Seven angels, dressed as priests, come from the temple ready to pour out final judgment (*15:6-8*).
- The first six bowls: God's righteous wrath (*16:1-16*).
  - ▶ **Bowl 1:** ugly and painful sores (*16:1-2*). This plague falls directly on those who worship the beast.
  - ▶ **Bowl 2:** the sea turns to blood (*16:3;* see *8:8*). Everything in the sea dies (See *Exo. 7:17-21*). In the trumpet plagues, only one-third of the sea turned to blood. In the bowls, judgment is final and complete.
  - ▶ **Bowl 3:** rivers and springs of water become blood (*16:4-7*). Like the third trumpet, this plague turns rivers and springs to blood (See *8:10-11*).
    - ▷ The "altar" speaks (*4:7*).
    - ▷ As the saints under the altar prayed in *6:9-10*, they now affirm that God's judgment is right.
  - ▶ **Bowl 4:** the sun scorches people (*16:8-9*). God overrules nature with scorching heat. Even so, those who are left in the world reject God (See *8:12*).
  - ▶ **Bowl 5:** darkness (*16:10-11*).
  - ▶ The angel pours this plague on the center of the beast's power. Still, followers of the beast refuse to repent.
    - ▷ This is the only time in the book of *Revelation* that "throne" does not refer to God's throne.[92]
  - ▶ **Bowl 6:** Euphrates River dries up (*16:12-16*). This bowl does not pour out a plague on humans. Drying up the river removes everything that holds back the "kings from the east." Nothing will stop the final battle between God and Satan.
    - ▷ *"frogs"* — an unclean animal (*16:13;* see *Lev. 11:10*).
    - ▷ *"battle"* — Armageddon (*16:14;* see *16:16; 19:17-21*).
    - ▷ *"blessed"* — the third blessing, or beatitude in *Revelation*. Jesus promises blessing to those who are spiritually watchful (*16:15*).
    - ▷ *"Armageddon"* — a famous battleground in the history of Israel. Some believe John means a physical place. Some believe this is a symbol of the final battle between God and Satan.[93] It seems to refer to the battleground in Israel, once referred to by France's General Napoleon as the finest battleground in the world.

How are the seven bowls similar to the seven seals and seven trumpets? Discuss.

NOTES

NOTES

- **The Seventh Bowl:** judgment on Babylon (*16:17-21*).
  - ▶ *"Into the air"* — Demons were thought to live in the air. God's power now attacks demons in their own territory (*17:17*).⁹⁴
  - ▶ *"Loud voice"* — God announces finished action. The judgment against Babylon is complete (*16:17*).
  - ▶ *"Babylon"* — Some believe this is Rome. It might also be a symbol for human civilization that rebels against God (*17:19*; see *11:8*).
    - ▷ *"divided into three parts"* — This means complete ruin.
    - ▷ *"fierceness of His wrath"* — God holds nothing back at this point.
- The scarlet woman and the beast (*17:1-18*).
  - ▶ John sees a drunken woman sitting on the beast (*17:1-6*).
    - ▷ *"fornication"* — In the Bible, this often is a symbol for idolatry and rebellion against God (*17:1-2*; see *Nah. 3:4* and the book of *Hosea* for examples).
    - ▷ *"scarlet beast"* — The description shows this is the same beast that rose from the sea (*17:3*; see *13:1, 5, 6*).

    "…and I saw a woman sitting on a scarlet beast which was full of names of blasphemy, having seven heads and ten horns" (*17:3*).

    - ▷ *"Arrayed in purple and scarlet…"* — The woman is dressed as a queen. We would expect something good from a cup of gold, but the cup holds filth (*17:4*).
    - ▷ *"drunk with the blood of the saints"* — The woman enjoyed killing believers (*17:6*).
  - ▶ The angel explains the vision (*17:7-14*).
    - ▷ *"was, and is not, and will ascend"* — (*17:8*). This calls to mind the description of the Lamb (*1:18; 2:8*). The beast imitates the power of Christ but is doomed. God's triumph is already sure.

    "The beast that you saw was, and is not, and will ascend out of the bottomless pit and go to perdition" (*17:8*).

    - ▷ *"seven mountains"* — This may refer to the traditional seven hills of Rome, and "Babylon" is a symbol of a series of Roman Emperors. Or, the mountains may be symbols of earthly empires. In John's time, people would think of Rome as the sixth major world empire.⁹⁵
    - ▷ *"also the eighth, and is of the seven"* — (*17:11*). The beast, the Antichrist, will play the role of a king. He is also separate because he is part of the great struggle between God and Satan.
    - ▷ *"ten kings"* — Earthly kings will be loyal to the beast. Ten may be a symbolic number to mean many.⁹⁶ The forces of evil unite. The kings fight on the beast's side in the battle against the Lamb, who is Christ (*17:12-13*; see *3:7; 19:19-21*).
  - ▶ The woman is punished (*17:15-18*).
    - ▷ *"hate the harlot"* — The loyalty of the beast will shift.
    - ▷ The beast and kings will destroy the woman.
    - ▷ God uses the beast to judge the woman, Babylon.

- Babylon the Great falls (*18:1–19:5*).
  ▶ An angel with great authority announces that Babylon has fallen. God triumphs (*18:1-3*).
  ▶ *"Come out of her"* — This is a common phrase in prophetic writings. God calls His people to be separate (*18:4-5;* see *Isa. 52:11; Jer. 51:45; 2 Cor. 6:17*).
  ▶ Judgment against Babylon is sure (*18:6-8*).
    ▷ Whether we interpret Babylon as the Roman Empire or the world in opposition to God, she will be punished.
    ▷ Babylon boasted and glorified herself. Now she faces the consequence of her sin.
  ▶ Three groups mourned for the woman Babylon and the evil she represented. This section is in the style of an ancient lament, such as Ezekiel's lament over the destruction of Tyre (*18:9-19;* see *Eze. 27*).
    ▷ *"kings of the earth"* — They stand far off in terror (*18:9-10*).
    ▷ *"merchants of the earth"* — They have a selfish motive because they will lose money. They also stand far off in terror (*18:11-17a*).
    ▷ *"every shipmaster"* — Those who make their living by shipping goods around the world (*18:17b-19*).
  ▶ The loud voice calls God's people to rejoice at the destruction of Babylon (*18:20;* see *19:1-5*).
  ▶ An angel throws a large millstone into the sea as an illustration of the fall of Babylon (*18:21*).
    ▷ Such a stone weighed thousands of pounds.
    ▷ Destruction is complete (*18:22-24*).

  "The sound of harpists, musicians, flutists, and trumpeters shall not be heard in you anymore. No craftsman of any craft shall be found in you anymore, and the sound of a millstone shall not be heard in you anymore. The light of a lamp shall not shine in you anymore, and the voice of the bridegroom and bride shall not be heard in you anymore" (*18:22-23*).

  ▶ A great multitude in heaven gives thanks for the destruction of Babylon (*19:1-5;* see *7:9*).
    ▷ *"Alleluia"* — the Hebrew word for "praise the Lord." It appears in the New Testament only in *Rev. 19:1, 3, 4, 6*.
    ▷ *"twenty-four elders and the four living creatures"* praise God for destroying Satan's power (See *4:2-11; 5:8-14; 11:16; 14:3*).

F. <u>The King of Kings Comes Again to Reign</u> (*19:6-20:15*)
- Praise for the marriage of the Lamb (*19:6-10*).

"Alleluia! For the Lord God Omnipotent reigns! Let us be glad and rejoice and give Him glory for the marriage of the Lamb has come and His wife has made herself ready. And to her it was granted to be arrayed in fine linen, clean and bright, for the fine linen is the righteous acts of the saints" (*19:6-8*).

NOTES

- ▶ The image of a wedding shows the close relationship between God and His people (See *Hos. 2:19-20; Eph. 5:23, 32*).
  - ▷ The bride got ready for the wedding with special treatments for her skin and hair.[97]
  - ▷ *"fine linen"* — The bride's pure clothing contrasts with the harlot's clothing in *17:4* and *18:16*.
- ▶ *"Blessed"* — The fourth beatitude (*19:9*).
- ▶ *"Marriage supper"* — joyous feasting by those who are faithful to Christ.
- ▶ John responds to the vision with worship. The angel tells him to worship only God (*19:10*).

Compare the joyous image of the wedding supper of the Lamb (*19:9*) with the gloomy picture of the supper of God (*19:17*). What does each mean for the believer? Discuss.

- John sees Christ on a white horse coming to defeat Satan (*19:11-21*).
  - ▶ White is a color of victory (This is probably not the same white horse of *6:2*; see *19:11*).
  - ▶ Christ is *"faithful and true."* Righteous judgment reflects a righteous God (*19:11*).
  - ▶ The description of Christ here is similar to the description in *1:14*. *"Many crowns"* means Christ is a king more powerful than Satan or the beast.[98]
  - ▶ *"Robe dipped in blood"* — This may mean Christ's blood on the cross or the blood of the enemy in the great conflict between the Lamb and the beast (*19:13*; see *14:14-20; Isa. 63:1-3*).
  - ▶ *"Armies in heaven"* — They wear white because they share in Christ's victory. These may be angels or believers (*19:14*; see *14:19-20; Deu. 33:2; Psa. 68:17*).
  - ▶ *"Sharp sword"* — Christ's only weapon is the sword mentioned in *1:16*.
  - ▶ *"King of kings"* — Christ the lamb is now supreme King (*19:16*; see *17:14*).
  - ▶ An angel calls birds to feast on the beast and his allies, who will soon be destroyed (*19:17-18*).
  - ▶ The beast and his armies gather. Immediately, Christ defeats them (*19:19-21*).
    - ▷ John does not describe a battle, only final defeat.
    - ▷ Both the beast and the false prophet (Antichrist) suffer defeat.
    - ▷ Christ throws them into the *"lake of fire burning with brimstone"* (*19:20*).
    - ▷ Christ slays the beast's armies (*19:21*).

- The millennial reign of Christ (*20:1-6*).
  - Christ has done away with the beast and the false prophet. Now Christ turns to Satan himself, the dragon (*20:2*).

  "Then I saw an angel coming down from heaven, having the key to the bottomless pit and a great chain in his hand. He laid hold of the dragon, that serpent of old, who is the Devil and Satan, and bound him for a thousand years; and he cast him into the bottomless pit, and shut him up, and set a seal on him, so that he should deceive the nations no more till the thousand years were finished. But after these things he must be released for a little while" (*20:1-3*).

  - *"Shut him up ... must be released"* — God has a plan even for Satan. Satan will not simply escape, but rather God will allow him to go.
  - *"Thousand years"* — This is the word that becomes "The Millennium." Many believe this to be 1,000 plain literal years.
  - *"Thrones"* — Believers reign with Christ for the "millennium." (*20:4;* see *Mat. 19:28; 1 Cor. 6:2.* Also see *Dan. 7:9-10, 22* for similarities to *Rev. 20*).
    - *"those who had been beheaded"* — martyrs killed by the beast (*13:7; 13:15*) and the victorious crowd (*15:2-4*). They may represent all who give their lives for Christ.
    - *"rest of the dead"* — This suggests that not everyone is raised at the start of the millennium. Rather, dead believers are raised. After the millennium, all people will be raised to face judgment (*20:5;* see *Dan. 12:2; Joh. 5:29; 1 Cor. 15:23; 1 Cor. 15:52*).
  - *"Blessed"* — the fifth beatitude (*20:6*).
  - *"Second death"* — eternal torment for unbelievers (*20:6;* see *2:11*).
  - Satan is destroyed (*20:7-10*).
  - Even after Christ has reigned 1,000 years, Satan finds people to deceive (*20:7-8*).
  - *"Gog and Magog"* — names in the Bible for nations who rebel against God (See *Eze. 38:1-39*).
  - Armies of the world gather for battle again (*20:9*).
  - John does not record a battle, only victory for Christ. Satan is thrown into the lake of fire. This is where the beast and false prophet are (*20:10;* see *19:20*).
- The great white throne judgment (*20:11-15*).
  - This is the final judgment. All people will stand before God.
    - The lost will be judged at the White Throne.
    - Believers will stand before the Judgment Seat of Christ (the bema) and receive rewards or lack of rewards for the life they lived in Christ (*2 Cor. 5:10*).

  "And they were judged, each one according to his works" (*20:13b*).

  - *"Books were opened"* — records of all the works people did during their lives (*20:12*).
  - *"Another book"* — The Book of Life is God's list of people who are saved.

NOTES

NOTES **What do you think is the relationship between these two kinds of books? Discuss.**

    G. <u>The New Heaven and Earth and the New Jerusalem</u> (*21:1-22:5*)
- The new eternal state (*21:1-8*).
  - ▶ *"New heaven and new earth"* — This fulfills Old Testament prophecies in *Isa. 65:17; Isa 66:22* and Peter's words in *2 Pet. 3:13*.
  - ▶ *"Tabernacle of God is with men"* — The New Jerusalem descends and God dwells with His people (*21:3*; see *Joh. 1:14; Rev. 7:15; Eze. 37:27-28*).
  - ▶ *"He who sat on the throne"* — God speaks. He makes a new creation with a final separation between good and evil (*21:5-8*).
- John sees the glory of New Jerusalem (*21:9-27*).
  - ▶ The main characteristic of the New Jerusalem is the glory of God (*21:11*).
  - ▶ *"Gold reed"* — In *Rev. 11*, measuring is for protection. Here measuring is to show the size and perfection of the city (*21:15*).

In this picture of heaven, what gives you the most encouragement?

- Pictures of an eternal Eden in the new creation (*22:1-5*).
  - ▶ *"Water of life"* — This image combines the Garden of Eden (*Gen. 2:8-14*) and the new temple Ezekiel saw (*Eze. 47:1-2*).
  - ▶ *"Tree of life"* — The first tree was in the Garden of Eden (*Gen. 3:22-24*). Ezekiel's tree bore fruit every month (*Eze. 17:12*).
  - ▶ *"They shall see His face"* — No human sees God's face before this time (*22:4*; see *1 Cor. 13:12; Exo. 33:20*).

4. Conclusion (*22:6-21*)

    A. <u>Jesus Assures Believers He Is Coming Soon</u> (*22:6-15*)
- *"Blessed"* — the sixth beatitude (*22:7*), and the seventh and final beatitude (*22:14-15*).
- Jesus makes clear the purpose of the revelation. John's visions should encourage the churches to hold fast to the truth (*22:16*).

    B. <u>Benediction: "Come, Lord Jesus"</u> (*22:20-21*)
- God's last message in the Bible (*22:17-21*).

NOTES

- The last invitation in the Bible (*22:17*).
  - The Spirit says *"Come."* The Holy Spirit calls people to come to Christ (See *Joh. 16:7-11*).
  - The bride says *"Come."* The bride refers to the true church (*Eph. 5:25-32*).
  - Those who hear say, *"Come."* Everyone who hears the message of Christ should call others to Him. We can begin this now.
- The last warning in the Bible (*22:18-19*).
  - This warning is about adding to the things written in the book of *Revelation* (*22:18*), or taking away from the things written in this book (*22:19*).
  - God's warnings apply to the whole Bible. God warns against taking or adding to His Word close to the beginning of the Bible (*Deu. 4:2*), near the middle of the Bible (*Pro. 30:6*), and here at the close (*Rev. 22:18-19*).
  - God warns about taking or adding from His Word.
- The last promise in the Bible (*22:20a*).
  - *"Surely I am coming quickly"* — Three times in that last chapter of the Bible Jesus promises to come back quickly. Elsewhere His coming is described as:
  - *"at hand"* (*Jas. 5:8*).
  - *"at the doors"* (*Mat. 24:33*).
  - *"yet a little while"* (*Heb. 10:37*).
  - *"in a moment"* (*1 Cor. 15:52*).
  - *"suddenly"* (*Mar. 13:36*).
- The last prayer in the Bible (*22:20b*).
  - After Jesus promised He would come quickly, John prayed, *"Even so, come, Lord Jesus."* John wanted Jesus to come.
  - The coming of Jesus is a comforting hope (*1 The. 4:16-18*), a blessed hope (*Tit. 2:13*) and a purifying hope (*1 Joh. 3:3*).

How does the book of *Revelation* relate to the life of the average believer?

If someone asked you to explain the book of *Revelation* in a simple way, what would you say? Discuss

Suggestions for Preaching From *Revelation*

- Apply the lessons of the letters to the seven churches to your setting.

- Use the pictures of the end of time to assure believers of God's work in the world and in their lives.

- Show how evil and injustice will not triumph forever and draw lessons for encouragement in life now.

CONCLUSION

God has a plan for human history. He has a plan for the salvation of humans. The Old Testament is full of promises that God would bring salvation to all people through the Jews. When Christ came as a man, God in human flesh, this plan for salvation moved forward. One day Christ will come again. At the end of time, Christ will rule in God's eternal kingdom.

Christians in the first century had many questions about God's plan. Some of these early believers were Jews, but they did not always understand the Old Testament Scriptures about the Messiah. Other believers were Gentiles who wanted to understand how they could know God.

The New Testament writers wrote letters to real people with real problems. False teachers were everywhere. Persecution was common. Rapid growth of the church brought many challenges. Relationships changed. Jewish leaders grew angry about this new religion. The Roman government grew hostile toward Christians. Though the first readers lived long ago, they were real people.

The letters of the New Testament served two purposes. First, they gave right teaching about God's work of salvation. They explained who Jesus Christ was and what His life, death and resurrection meant. Their writing extended a more complete theology and a new kind of relationship with God. No longer are we separated from God. We are united to Christ. God's Spirit lives in us.

Second, the letters gave right teaching about holy living. Life takes on new meaning as we live in grace, the way God means for us to live. In the New Testament, God creates a new people — believers who are both Jews and Gentiles. The church is the body of Christ. The church is the presence of Christ in the world. When we understand our identity, we answer God's call to be a new people in all our relationships. The mark of God's people is love. Paul and the other writers of the New Testament stress that the evidence of our faith is in our actions.

Our new relationship with God begins with "justification," when God declares us not guilty because of Christ's sacrifice. It continues in "sanctification" as we become holy in our ordinary relationships and decisions. Christ's death gives us the free gift of eternal life, but it calls us to live with a new commitment to His grace and power. This commitment shows in our daily lives. Finally, Christ's death and resurrection point us to our future "glorification," when we ourselves will be resurrected. When Jesus comes again, He will set up God's kingdom for eternity.

In the New Testament, God redeems His people and the world. God shows that He has been in control of history since the start of time. Christ is not just a King, but the King of kings. These are the themes of Paul and the other writers. All who believe may experience God's salvation, a new life of holiness in the Spirit, and eternity in God's kingdom.

We are becoming today by what we do with what we have, what we will be in the life to come!

ENDNOTES

Introduction
[1] These dates are based on information in separate book introductions by Earl D. Radmacher, general editor, *Nelson's New Illustrated Bible Commentary* (Nashville: Thomas Nelson, 1999).

Romans
[2] Earl D. Radmacher, General Editor, *The Nelson Study Bible New King James Version* (Nashville: Thomas Nelson Bibles, 1997) 1900.
[3] Earl D. Radmacher, General Editor, *Nelson's New Illustrated Bible Commentary* (Nashville: Thomas Nelson, 1999) 1449.

1 Corinthians
[4] John F. Walvoord and Roy B. Zuck, editors, *The Bible Knowledge Commentary New Testament Edition* (Colorado Springs: Victor Books, 2004) 529.
[5] Kenneth L. Barker, general editor, *New International Study Bible* (Grand Rapids: Zondervan), 1476.
[6] *New International Study Bible*, 1795.

2 Corinthians
[7] *New Illustrated Bible Commentary*, 1497.
[8] *New Illustrated Bible Commentary*, 1505.
[9] *New Illustrated Bible Commentary*, 1511.

Galatians
[10] *New Illustrated Bible Commentary*, 1514–1515.
[11] *New Illustrated Bible Commentary*, 1514.
[12] *New Illustrated Bible Commentary*, 1520,
[13] *New Illustrated Bible Commentary*, 1522
[14] *Bible Knowledge Commentary*, 604.

Ephesians
[15] *Nelson Study Bible*, 1981-82.
[16] *New Illustrated Bible Commentary*, 1533.
[17] *Nelson Study Bible*, 1983.
[18] *New Illustrated Bible Commentary*, 1534.
[19] *Nelson Study Bible*, 1988.
[20] *New Illustrated Bible Commentary*, 1539.
[21] *Nelson Study Bible*, 1992.
[22] *Nelson Study Bible*, 1992; New International Version Study Bible, 1840.

Philippians
[23] *New Illustrated Bible Commentary*, 1543-45.
[24] *Nelson Study Bible New King James Version*, 1997.
[25] *Nelson Study Bible*, 1998.
[26] *Nelson Study Bible*, 1999.
[27] *Nelson Study Bible*, 2000.
[28] *New Illustrated Bible Commentary*, 1551.
[29] *New Illustrated Bible Commentary*, 1551
[30] *Nelson Study Bible*, 2004.

Colossians
[31] *Nelson Study Bible New King James Version*, 2008.

1 Thessalonians
[32] *New International Study Bible*, 1862.
[33] *New Illustrated Bible Commentary*, 1576.
[34] *New International Version Study Bible*, 1863.

[35] *Nelson Study Bible*, 2026.
[36] *New Illustrated Bible Commentary*, 1577.
[37] *New International Version Study Bible*, 1864.
[38] F. F. Bruce, 1 & 2 Thessalonians (*Word Biblical Commentary*, vol. 45; Waco Texas, Word Books, 1982) 91.
[39] Bruce, 125.
[40] *Nelson Study Bible*, 2030.

2 Thessalonians
[41] *New International Version Study Bible*, 1868
[42] *New International Version Study Bible*, 1969 and *Nelson Study Bible*, 2034.
[43] *New Illustrated Bible Commentary*, 1588.

Philemon
[44] *New Illustrated Bible Commentary*, 1628.
[45] *New Illustrated Bible Commentary*, 1631.

Hebrews
[46] *New Illustrated Bible Commentary*, 1640.
[47] *New International Version Study Bible*, 1896.
[48] *Nelson Study Bible*, 2080.
[49] *Nelson Study Bible*, 2081
[50] F.F. Bruce, The Epistles to the Hebrews (*New International Commentary of the New Testament*, Grand Rapids: Eerdmans) 68.
[51] *New International Version Study Bible*, 1901.
[52] Ronald F. Youngblood, general editor, *Nelson's New Illustrated Bible Dictionary* (Nashville: Thomas Nelson, 1995) 1026–27.
[53] *New Illustrated Bible Commentary*, 1644.
[54] *New Illustrated Bible Commentary*, 1646.
[55] Colin Brown, general editor, *The New International Dictionary of New Testament Theology* (Grand Rapids: Zondervan, 1971) vol. III, 604.
[56] *New International Version Study Bible*, 1913.
[57] *New Illustrated Bible Commentary*, 2099.
[58] *New Illustrated Bible Commentary*, 2100.

James
[59] *New Illustrated Bible Commentary*, 2118.
[60] *New International Bible Commentary*, 1662.
[61] *Bible Knowledge Commentary*, 822.
[62] *Bible Knowledge Commentary*, 823.
[63] *New International Version Study Bible*, 1921.

1 Peter
[64] *New International Version Study Bible*, 1930.
[65] *Nelson Study Bible*, 2120.
[66] *Nelson Study Bible*, 2123.
[67] *New International Version Study Bible*, 1933.
[68] *Nelson Study Bible*, 2123.
[69] ibid.

2 Peter
[70] *Bible Knowledge Commentary*, 868-869.

1 John
[71] *Nelson Study Bible*, 2144.

Jude
[72] *New International Version Study Bible*, 1960.
[73] *New International Version Study Bible*, 1961.

Revelation

[74] *New International Version Study Bible*, 1966.
[75] *Nelson Study Bible*, 2166
[76] *New International Version Study Bible*, 1964.
[77] *New International Version Study Bible*, 1969.
[78] *New International Version Study Bible*, 1970.
[79] *New International Version Study Bible*, 1970.
[80] *New Illustrated Bible Commentary*, 1742.
[81] *New International Version Study Bible*, 1971.
[82] *New International Version Study Bible*, 1973.
[83] *Bible Knowledge Commentary*, 949.
[84] *New International Version Study Bible*, 1974.
[85] *Bible Knowledge Commentary*, 950.
[86] *New International Version Study Bible*, 1978; *Nelson Study Bible*, 2182.
[87] *New Illustrated Bible Commentary*, 1750.
[88] *New International Version Study Bible*, 1980; *New Illustrated Bible Commentary*, 1953.
[89] *New Illustrated Bible Commentary*, 1753.
[90] *Bible Knowledge Commentary*, 964.
[91] *New International Version Study Bible*, 1981
[92] *New Illustrated Bible Commentary*, 1756.
[93] *New Illustrated Bible Commentary*, 1757.
[94] Leon Morris, *The Revelation of St. John* (Grand Rapid: Eerdmans, The Tyndale Press, 1969) 200.
[95] *New Illustrated Bible Commentary*, 1759.
[96] *New International Version Study Bible*, 1985
[97] *New Illustrated Bible Commentary*, 1761.
[98] *New Illustrated Bible Commentary*, 1761.